W9-BBA-715

THE RESTORATION OF THAILAND UNDER RAMA I 1782–1809

The Association for Asian Studies: Monographs and Papers, No. XXIV
Paul Wheatley, *Editor*

THE RESTORATION OF THAILAND UNDER RAMA I 1782-1809

BY KLAUS WENK

TRANSLATED FROM THE GERMAN
BY GREELEY STAHL

Published for The Association for Asian Studies by
THE UNIVERSITY OF ARIZONA PRESS · TUCSON

About the Author . . .

KLAUS WENK has a scholarly background in both the literary and civil history and traditions of Thailand. He is the author of several studies in the German language on Thai laws and civil process. He holds the degrees of LL.B. in law and Ph.D. in Asiatic studies from the University of Hamburg, and has had published a number of monographs and articles on the poetry, prose, and fine arts of the Thai people. He studied at Chulalongkon University in Bangkok and spent two years traveling in Southeast Asia, visiting Laos, Cambodia, Malaysia, Indonesia, and India before joining the faculty at Hamburg to teach Southeast Asian languages and cultures.

Publication of this volume has been
made possible by a generous grant to
The Association for Asian Studies
by the Ford Foundation.

Library of Congress Catalog
Card No. 67–63491

หนังสือเล่มนี้
ขอถวาย

แด่
พระวรวงศ์เธอกรมหมื่นพิทยลาพฤฒิยากร
พระองค์เจ้าธานีนิวัติ
ผู้ทรงคุณวุฒิยิ่งทั้งทางฝ่าย
การเมืองและการศึกษา

MONOGRAPHS AND PAPERS OF THE ASSOCIATION FOR ASIAN STUDIES

I. *Money Economy in Medieval Japan,* by Delmer M. Brown. Locust Valley, New York: J. J. Augustin, 1951. $2.50

II. *China's Management of the American Barbarians,* by Earl Swisher. J. J. Augustin, 1951. $7.50

III. *Leadership and Power in the Chinese Community of Thailand,* by G. William Skinner. Cornell University Press, 1958. $6.50

IV. *Siam Under Rama III, 1824–1851,* by Walter F. Vella. J. J. Augustin, 1957. $5.00

V. *The Rise of the Merchant Class in Tokugawa Japan: 1600–1868,* by Charles David Sheldon. J. J. Augustin, 1958. $5.00

VI. *Chinese Secret Societies in Malaya,* by L. F. Comber. J. J. Augustin, 1959. $6.50

VII. *The Traditional Chinese Clan Rules,* by Hui-chen Wang Liu. J. J. Augustin, 1959. $5.50

VIII. *A Comparative Analysis of the Jajmani System,* by Thomas O. Beidelman. J. J. Augustin, 1959. $2.50

IX. *Colonial Labor Policy and Administration,* by J. Norman Parmer. J. J. Augustin, 1959. $6.00

X. *Bankguad—A Community Study in Thailand,* by Howard Keva Kaufman. J. J. Augustin: 1959. $5.50

XI. *Agricultural Involution: The Processes of Ecological Change in Indonesia,* by Clifford Geertz. The University of California Press, 1963. $4.00

XII. *Maharashta Purana,* by Edward C. Dimock, Jr., and Pratul Chandra. Honolulu: The East-West Center Press, 1964. $5.00

XIII. *Conciliation in Japanese Legal Practice,* by Dan Fenno Henderson. The University of Washington Press, 1964.

XIV. *The Malayan Tin Industry to 1914,* by Wong Lin Ken. The University of Arizona Press, 1965. $6.50

XV. *Reform, Rebellion, and the Heavenly Way,* by Benjamin F. Weems. The University of Arizona Press, 1964. $3.75

XVI. *Korean Literature: Topics and Themes,* by Peter H. Lee. The University of Arizona Press, 1965. $3.75

XVII. *Ch'oe Pu's Diary: A Record of Drifting Across the Sea,* by John Meskill. The University of Arizona Press, 1965. $4.50

XVIII. *The British in Malaya: The First Forty Years,* by K. G. Tregonning. The University of Arizona Press, 1965. $4.50

XIX. *Chiaraijima Village: Land Tenure, Taxation, and Local Trade,* by William Chambliss. The University of Arizona Press, 1965. $5.00

XX. *Shinran's Gospel of Pure Grace,* by Alfred Bloom. The University of Arizona Press, 1965. $5.00

XXI. *Before Aggression: Europeans Prepare the Japanese Army,* by Ernst L. Presseisen. The University of Arizona Press, 1965. $5.00

XXII. *A Documentary Chronicle of Sino-Western Relations: 1644–1820,* by Lo-shu Fu. The University of Arizona Press, 1966. xviii + 792 pp. $14.50

XXIII. *K'ang Yu-Wei: A Biography and a Symposium,* edited by Lo Jung-pang. The University of Arizona Press, 1967. 541 pp. $14.50

XXIV. *The Restoration of Thailand Under Rama I: 1782–1809,* by Klaus Wenk. The University of Arizona Press, 1968. 150 pp. $7.50

CONTENTS

PREFACE

THE PRESENT WORK is concerned essentially with the political history of Thailand at the end of the eighteenth and the beginning of the nineteenth century. The weight of emphasis in the account varies according to the available sources of information. In general, this account may be considered as a preliminary study to be followed later by a general study of the modern history of Thailand, a subject which cannot be adequately handled without further preparatory investigations.[1] Even the treatment of a limited period of time as in the present work is not without risk. For a number of particular questions, adequate preparatory work has not yet been undertaken.

The words "according to Thai sources of information" would be appropriate under the title of this study. European literature concerning the time of Rama I is exceedingly limited and is concerned only with secondary questions or very general subjects of investigation. The flood of European accounts does not begin until the time of Rama III.[2] Although in these accounts there is undoubtedly a good deal to be found which is useful for the study of the time of Rama I, we have, nevertheless, made no attempt to evaluate this literature in the present study. As research in the modern history of Thailand is still in its elementary stage, the primary need at the moment is to ascertain what can be definitely established from direct sources of information.

A revision of certain details of this history will perhaps be in order

[1] Hall's *A History of Southeast Asia* shows this very clearly. Although this work is only of summary character, it nevertheless contains a large number of inaccuracies and mistakes, at least for the period 1782–1809 which is treated in the present study. As Hall does not give specific references in support of his statements, we say nothing more about this matter.

[2] On this point see the excellent study by Vella, *Siam under Rama III, 1824–1851*.

when the primary historical documents of neighboring states, particularly Burma and Vietnam, are made available to us and are examined with the same degree of care and attention. A scientific evaluation of the presently available material from these countries in connection with the history of Thailand is now possible only to a limited extent.

In the present monograph the following material has not been taken into consideration: (1) The literature of the court of Rama I, which at this time reached one of its highest peaks in Thailand. Putting the whole gigantic complex of the Ramakien in proper order with regard to both the text itself and its place in literary history would itself be the work of a lifetime. As a beginning one may refer to the accounts in the general histories of literature. (2) The revision of the Buddhist Canon of 1788 at the Bangkok Council. Whether the texts used at that time provide satisfactory research material, and, if so, to what extent, I do not know. At best, such material would probably not amount to anything more than remnants of manuscripts which can be dated with certainty. (3) The new codification of the Ayuthaya laws. Problems concerning this are treated to some extent in the following monograph, to which reference can be made. The disclosure of this codex, now available, with its 1416 pages in the form of a dictionary, should be one of the principal tasks of future research in Thai studies. The revised codex of 1805 is virtually the only source of information for research on political and sociological conditions in Thailand until the time of Rama I.

On the other hand, many details have been included in this account, which normally would be beyond the scope of a historical study, in order to throw some light on the sociological background of the history of Thailand, which, generally speaking, is scarcely known in outline. At the same time it is one of the purposes of this study to call attention to the richness of material in Thai historical sources which is still awaiting disclosure.

The history of neighboring and border states has been treated only as far as the relations between Thailand and these countries made this necessary and only to the extent that Thai sources of information add to our knowledge. This is particularly true in the cases of Laos, Cambodia and Vietnam. For the balance reference was made to the available Western literature.

One more observation regarding source material: The principal source of information for the history of Rama I is the *Phraratcha Phongsawadan ratchakan thi nüng* by Čau Phraya Thiphakarawong.

This work was completed around 1869,[3] but was not published at that time. It was not until 1902 that Prince Damrong was commissioned by Čulalongkǫn, Rama V, to examine the handwritten volumes[4] and prepare them for publication. Damrong states that the work of Thiphakarawong appears to be based on an earlier work of Krom Somdet Phra Bǫrǫmanuchit Chinorot and that he himself has corrected and completed the manuscript of Thiphakarawong partly on the basis of other handwritten works and partly on the basis of printed works (which however are not mentioned by name). Further information is not available at present. The main body of the remaining authoritative source material is to be found in the "Collection of Historical Sources," *Prachum Phongsawadan*, the bibliography of which has already been considered elsewhere.[5]

The transliteration used in the text of the present study follows, with a few slight variations, the system proposed by the Royal Institute of Thailand.[6] The spoken word is transliterated irrespective of the orthography of the Thai phrases and tones. Only exceptionally are concessions made to a transliteration which is commonly acknowledged and in use, especially the duplication of consonants as in *-thamm* or *sawann*, for example.

Finally, I should like to express my gratitude to both Professor George Coedès of Paris and Professor Walter Vella of the University of Hawaii for the valuable suggestions that they made during the course of this work, and to the University of Arizona Press for bringing about publication.

Klaus Wenk

[3] See the preface to the edition of the *Phraratcha Phongsawadan ratchakan thi nüng* used in the present study, henceforth abbreviated as Thiphakarawong *P.P.R.I.*

[4] *Samut thai;* according to the statements of Damrong there were twelve of them in the Royal Library.

[5] Wenk, "Prachum Phongsāwadān . . . ," pp. 232 *et seq.;* and partly in Vella, *Siam under Rama III, 1824–1851*, pp. 148–156.

[6] *Journal of the Siam Society*, vol. 33, pp. 49 *et seq.*

Chapter I

THE BEGINNING OF THE ČAKRI DYNASTY

WE HAVE VERY LITTLE authentic information about the origin of the Čakri dynasty. Moreover, we can be reasonably sure that no additional source material will be discovered. An examination of existing evidence makes it very clear that the genealogy of the Čakri family generally accepted today is essentially based only on the statements of Mongkut, Rama IV, to Sir John Bowring.[1]

The family of Rama I can perhaps be traced back to the time of Phra Narai,[2] to a certain Čau Phraya Kosathibǫdi who was dispatched to the court of Louis XIV in 1688 as envoy of Phra Narai.[3] His son Khun Thǫng was nominated Phraya Wǫrawongsathirat under Phra Phutha Čau Sŭa. His son, in turn, became Phraratchanikun, whose son was Thǫngdi, the father of Rama I.

Thǫngdi, under Phra Čau Yu Hua Bǫrǫmakot, was appointed to *samientra*[4] with the title Phra Aksǫn Sunthǫnsat.[5] Later he received the title Čau Phraya Čakri Ǫngkharak and was in the service of the governor of Phitsanulok. As Phraya Aksǫn Sunthǫnsat, the father of Rama I had already married Dau Rŭang,[6] who apparently was descended from

[1] As reported in Bowring, *The Kingdom and the People of Siam*, vol. 1, pp. 63 *et seq.*; see also *Pathom wong*, pp. 76 *et seq.*

[2] Phitsanakha, *Prawatsat kasat thai*, pp. 10 *et seq.*; Sonakun, *Prawatsat Thai samai krung ratanakosin yuk raek*, pp. 3 *et seq.* The statements of Chakrabongse, *Lords of Life*, pp. 80 *et seq.*, appear to be speculative, according to our present knowledge, and for this reason cannot be discussed here; the same can be said for the declarations of Mongkut who locates the origins of his family at Pegu in the first half of the sixteenth century, in Bowring, *op. cit.*, p. 63.

[3] Bowring, *op. cit.*, p. 64; see also vols. 57–60 of Prachum Phongsawadan, *Kosapan pai Farangset.*

[4] Royal secretary of high rank.

[5] Or, as Phitsanaka, *op. cit.*, p. 11, says, Luong Phinitaksǫn.

[6] "Famous star."

a rich Chinese family from Ayuthaya.[7] Of this marriage there were five children, three sons and two daughters, as follows:[8]

1. Daughter Sa, later known as Krom Phra Thep Sadawadi Phra Phi Nang Tamnak Khwa.
2. Son Narong, who died in his youth.
3. Daughter Kaeo, later known as Krom Phra Si Sudarak Phra Phi Nang Tamnak Daeng.
4. Son Thǫng Duong, the future Rama I, who therefore was half Chinese by birth.
5. Son Bunma, the future Maha Uparat.

The birth of Thǫng Duong is variously given as 1736[9] or 1737,[10] and is today associated with a garland of "wonderful tales."[11]

After the death of Dau Rŭang, Thǫngdi married her younger sister, Tǫng Yok, who however died shortly after the birth of her daughter, Ku, later known as Krom Luong Narinthewi.[12] Of the following marriage of Thǫngdi with the third sister of Dau Rŭang there was a son, La, later known as Krom Luong Čakaračetsada.

When he was six years old Thǫng Duong was sent to the court at Ayuthaya, where, after two years, he became a page of the third son of King Bǫrǫmakot, Čau Fa Uthumphǫn Khun Phǫraphinit, at whose court Taksin, two years older, was also a page at this time.[13] The two young pages became very good friends, and at the ages of eleven and thirteen, respectively, became novices (*nen*) in Wat Sam Wihan in Ayuthaya. Thǫng Duong was later ordained in Wat Maha Thalai. In 1757 he gave up the monastic life and resumed service under Čau Fa Uthumphǫn. One year later King Bǫrǫmakot died and the Maha Uparat, Čau Fa Uthumphǫn, became the new king; however, he abdicated a few days later. Phra Thinang Suriyamarinthara, the last king of the Ayuthaya epoch, then took over the government. Under his reign

[7] According to what Mongkut said to Bowring, *op. cit.*, pp. 66 *et seq.* (The "list of princes and princesses" mentioned in Chakrabongse, *op. cit.*, p. 72, was not available to the author, but it also indicates that Dau Rŭang was of Chinese descent.)

[8] *Ratchasakunwong*, pp. 1 *et seq.*; *Pathom wong*, pp. 80 *et seq.*

[9] *P.P.R.I*, p. 353, gives Wednesday, the fifth day of the waning moon of the fourth lunar month in the year 2278 of the Buddhist era (March 22, 1736); Phitsanakha, *op. cit.*, p. 11, and Mongkut in Bowring, *op. cit.*, p. 66, give the same date.

[10] Chakrabongse, *op. cit.*, p. 72.

[11] As reported in Phitsanakha, *op. cit.*, pp. 12 *et seq.*

[12] The author of *Čotmaihet khuam songčam.*

[13] According to Phitsanakha, *op. cit.*, p. 16.

Thọng Duong at the age of 26 or 28[14] was nominated *Luong Yokrabat*[15] and was assigned to the governor of Ratburi, in whose service he entered. There he married Nak, the daughter of a prosperous family, and had his residence in Pang Chang in the vicinity of Samut Songkhram.[16]

In 1767, therefore, the future king of the country was not in Ayuthaya, and did not participate in the struggle against the Burmese. Before the fall of the city his brother Bunma, the future Maha Uparat, was able to flee to Pang Chang. Other members of the immediate family, parents, brothers and sisters, were also able to escape from the clutch of the Burmese, that is to say, from the possibility of being abducted to Burma. Bunma embarked from Samut Songkhram in the direction of Chonburi, without however having been able to persuade Thọng Duong to do the same thing.[17] Bunma was nominated as Phra Maha Montri Čau Phraya Tamruot Khwa[18] by Taksin, who was assembling his army at Chonburi.

Thọng Duong joined the army of Taksin before its decampment and was nominated by Taksin as Phra Ratcharin Čau Krom Phra Tamruot.[19] In the following fifteen years the future Rama I took part in eleven campaigns which furthered the liberation of the country from Burmese domination. In the last campaigns under Taksin, Phra Ratcharin was already the commander-in-chief of the belligerent armies. The following specific dates are known:[20]

1. In 1767 Phra Ratcharin, in attendance on Phraya Wọrawongsuthirat, fought with him in order to take Dankhunthot in the region of Nakhọn Ratchasima and then Siem Reap. During the operation on the Korat plateau, Phra Ratcharin was nominated Phraya Aphairanarit.[21]
2. In 1768 Phraya Aphairanarit was already commander of a unit in Cambodia and fought against Cambodian units in

[14] *P.P.R.I*, p. 353; *P.P.*, p. 472; Phitsanakha, *op. cit.*, pp. 24 and 26.
[15] A functionary who had the duties of a public prosecutor.
[16] Phitsanakha, *op. cit.*, p. 23; *P.P.R.I*, p. 353; *Pathom wong*, pp. 96 *et seq.*
[17] Phitsanakha, *op. cit.*, p. 25.
[18] Title of a high police functionary.
[19] Title as given in footnote 18.
[20] As specified in *P.P.R.I*, pp. 354 *et seq.* and in *P.P.*, pp. 472 *et seq.*
[21] For general information concerning titles see particularly Damrong, *Winichai phra yot*, pp. 1 *et seq.;* Damrong, *Wadui yot čau*, pp. 77 *et seq.;* Damrong, *Tamnan wang na*, pp. 1 *et seq.;* Čulalongkọn, *Phraratchawitčan*, pp. 246 *et seq.;* Sommot Amọraphan, *Chaloem phra yot čau nai;* Sommot Amọraphan, *Song tang phra bọrọmawongsanuwong;* Sommot Amọraphan, Tang čau phrayot; Quaritch-Wales, *Ancient Siamese Government and Administration*, pp. 22 *et seq.*

the region of Battambang and Siem Reap. During these operations he received news of the alleged death of Taksin and immediately withdrew his troops.

3. In 1769 he accompanied Taksin on the expedition for the subjection of the prince of Fang, and, after this campaign, received the title of Phraya Yomarat in the capacity of Samuhanayok.[22]
4. In 1770 Phraya Yomarat was named Phraya Čakri and troop commander so that he and his commander-in-chief, Taksin, could subjugate Cambodia. The cities of Banthaiphet and Baphnom were taken.
5. In 1773 Phraya Čakri was commander-in-chief of the troops operating in northern Thailand and took Chiengmai, Lampang and Lamphun, and once again subjugated Nan.
6. In the same year he warded off an attack of the Burmese on Ratburi, where he had led the army in a forced march from Chiengmai.
7. In 1774 Phraya Čakri advanced once again toward Chiengmai in order to stop a new Burmese invasion. There was, however, no battle, as the Burmese army withdrew after it received news of the arrival of Phraya Čakri.
8. Apparently in the same year,[23] the Burmese, under Asaewunki, once again invaded northern Thailand with armed forces greatly superior to those of the Thai troops. Phitsanulok was for some length of time under siege and was finally taken by the Burmese. The troops under the leadership of Phraya Čakri were not able to prevent the unfavorable course of the campaign[24] and withdrew eastward toward Phetchabun. However, during the course of the siege a personal meeting between the two enemy commanders did take place at the request of Asaewunki.[25]
9. In 1775 Phraya Čakri was the commander of an army which once again brought southern Laos into Thai possession. He took the districts and cities of Čampasak, Sithandọn and Atapŭ, as well as a number of the smaller

[22] Title of one of the highest government officials of the time with approximately the duties of a minister.

[23] See Damrong, *Thai rop Phama*, vol. 2, pp. 80 *et seq.*

[24] *P.P.R.I*, p. 356.

[25] Chakrabongse, *op. cit.*, p. 75.

northern Khmer cities. After this campaign Phraya Čakri became Čau Phraya[26] Maha Kasatsŭkphilŭkmahima Thuknakhararaădet Naresuonratchasuriyawong Ǫngbatmunlikakǫn Bǫwǫnratanaprinayok.

10. In 1777 Čau Phraya Maha Kasatsŭk undertook a campaign to Upper Laos. Vientiane and other Lao dominions as well as Luong Phra Bang again became subject to Thailand.
11. In 1781 the future king carried out his last campaign before his ascension to the throne. Revolts in Cambodia provided him with a new opportunity to march in with a larger army. Nevertheless, before the beginning of the intended hostilities the news reached him that unrest and trouble had arisen in Thonburi around Taksin. Maha Kasatsŭk immediately returned with his troops to Thonburi, where he arrived on the ninth day of the waning moon in the fifth lunar month of 2324 (1781).

The following events are among the most discussed and most controversial themes of modern Thai history, owing to the fact that they have been played up for political reasons. The result is known and beyond dispute: Taksin, the liberator of Thailand from the Burmese yoke, was dethroned and shortly afterwards put to death. Next, Čau Phraya Maha Kasatsŭk ascended to the throne of Thailand as the new king.

Contemporary material bearing on these events is not very informative, and this situation has favored politically inspired speculations and statements[27] which however are not historically justified.

Within the framework of this monograph it is impossible to discuss everything that happened regarding Taksin,[28] but only matters relevant to the behavior of Rama I.

The revolt against Taksin had its origin in the person of Phraya Sankhaburi,[29] one of Taksin's military commanders. The king, under siege in his own palace, abdicated and took monastic orders. The

[26] As *Čau Phraya* he had attained to the highest civil rank.

[27] Particularly after the coup d'état of 1932. For detailed information consult Vella, "The Impact of the West on the Government of Thailand," pp. 366 *et seq.*, where references about this may be obtained.

[28] More particulars are given in Ïeyaming-Phitsanakha, *Phra Čau Taksin Maharat.* Other scholarly biographies of Taksin are not yet available as far as the author knows.

[29] *Phraratcha Phongsawadan Krung Thonburi*, pp. 202 *et seq.*, 205; Ïeyaming-Phitsanakha, *op. cit.*, pp. 417 *et seq.;* Chakrabongse, *op. cit.*, p. 78; Wood, *A History of Siam*, pp. 270 *et seq.*

governor of Nakhǫn Ratchasima, Čau Phraya Maha Kasatsŭk, who was stationed with his troops at Siem Reap, received news of the events in Thonburi through Phraya Suriyāaphai. He then ordered Phraya Suriyāaphai to advance immediately to Thonburi. After a struggle the latter succeeded in taking the city[30] and putting an end to possible intentions of Phraya Sankhaburi regarding the throne of Thailand. Soon afterwards Čau Phraya Maha Kasatsŭk also came to Thonburi. The body of generals and officials assembled there immediately gave him their allegiance, and, after taking counsel in assembly, asked him to reign over the land as the new king.[31] On April 6, 1782, Čau Phraya Maha Kasatsŭk accepted this proposal and governed the country as Rama I[32] until his death in 1809.

No further information can be obtained from available sources. However, what we do know should justify the conclusion that the first sovereign of the Čakri dynasty ascended to the vacant throne of Thailand in a legitimate way.[33] In view of the predominant position which Rama I already had in the state, even before the abdication of Taksin, it was only natural that the crown should be offered to him rather than to one of the ambitious generals around Taksin. Not one case of disloyalty is known to us during the fifteen-year period when Rama I served as officer under Taksin. Moreover, the fact has been clearly established that the fall of Taksin was not brought about by Rama I.[34] This is of decisive importance in this discussion. The question whether Rama I welcomed the fall of Taksin either for personal or political reasons and, if so, to what extent, is beyond the scope of historical investigation and is of a purely speculative nature.

Today, from our perspective, there still remains the very theoretical question whether Čau Phraya Maha Kasatsŭk, upon his arrival in

[30] *Phraratcha Phongsawadan Krung Thonburi*, pp. 206 *et seq.*

[31] *P.P.R.I*, p. 357; *P.P.*, p. 476; Phitsanakha, *op. cit.*, p. 33; detailed references are in *Phraratcha Phongsawadan Krung Thonburi*, pp. 209 *et seq.;* Launay, *Histoire de la Mission de Siam*, vol. 2, p. 310, but see footnote 37 of this chapter.

[32] The designation of the Thai kings as Rama I, Rama II, etc., was first introduced by Wachirawut, Rama VI, and even today is unusual in Thailand, generally speaking. In contemporary sources, for example, Thiphakarawong, the king is designated by his title Phra Bat Somdet Bǫrǫmbǫphit Phra Čau Yu Hua or in a similar way. In this connection attention must be called to the fact that the title in this form was first put forward by Mongkut, Rama IV. The usual designation today of Rama I, Phra Phutha Yǫt Fa Čulalok, is only the name of the statue of the king in the royal pantheon in Wat Phra Kaeo.

[33] And not as a usurper as concluded by Robert-Martignan, *La Monarchie Absolue Siamoise de 1350 à 1925*, p. 181.

[34] At any rate, the source material does not provide any statements to support this idea.

Thonburi, had an obligation to restore the *status quo*, that is to say, to work for the restitution of Taksin. This question cannot be answered from the *Phra Thammasat*,[35] in any case not in accordance with the methodology which is demanded for the interpretation of the Thai laws.[36] In reality this matter is primarily not a legal but rather a political or even a moral question, to which it is virtually impossible to give an answer on a purely objective basis, as contemporary source material does not provide detailed information. From the viewpoint of the political observer the question may be answered with a categorical "no." A king more or less insane[37] who had abdicated, a mutinous body of generals in a country whose borders were seriously threatened from all sides, and finally the demand on the part of the great majority of the ruling classes that he should ascend to the throne, was the situation which confronted Čau Phraya Maha Kasatsŭk. If he had acted in any other way in such a situation, his behavior would have been considered unstatesmanlike and politically irresponsible. The question of the succession to the throne of one of the sons of Taksin may be answered from the same viewpoint.[38]

Taksin was the prisoner of the new king, a situation which for the latter was probably even less agreeable than for the prisoner himself, a monarch who had abdicated in a country which during the past hundred years had already had enough disorder in its dynasty. In an assembly the councilors of the king demanded the death penalty for Taksin,[39] calling attention to his misdeeds[40] during the last years of his reign. According to our sources, Rama I acceded to this demand and

[35] *Pramuon kotmai ratchakan thi nŭng*, vol. 1, pp. 4–34.

[36] There could be no greater methodological error than to attempt an interpretation of the old Thai royal laws with Western, logical ways of thinking.

[37] It seems clear that Taksin had fallen into a kind of Caesar complex. For this matter see particularly the accounts of the Jesuit fathers in Bangkok at that time as given in Launay, *Histoire de la Mission de Siam, 1662–1811*, vol. 2, p. 309; and in *Siam et les Missionaires Français*, pp. 162 *et seq.*, by the same author. Launay's account, to be sure, must be treated with some caution. He appears to be not entirely free of bias in favor of Rama I, who is referred to as "our king" (*Histoire de la Mission de Siam*, p. 321); the dubious statements relative to Kedah must also be considered in this light, see p. 105; also compare Phitsanakha, *op. cit.*, p. 34; Ĭeyaming-Phitsanakha, *op. cit.*, pp. 417 *et seq.;* Wood, *op. cit.*, p. 267, and the references cited in footnote 39.

[38] See on this point the Kot Monthienban, *Pramuon kotmai ratchakan thi nŭng*, vol. 1, pp. 58–129; and Quaritch-Wales, *Ancient Siamese Government and Administration*, pp. 19 *et seq.*

[39] *Phraratcha Phongsawadan Krung Thonburi*, pp. 210 *et seq.; P.P.*, pp. 189 *et seq.*

[40] Enumerated in *Phraratcha Phongsawadan Krung Thonburi*, pp. 210 *et seq.*, and in Phitsanakha, *op. cit.*, p. 34.

ordered the execution of Taksin. Before this was carried out the prisoner asked the executioner to arrange for an audience with the new king. Rama I gave a sign of refusal but with tears running down his face.[41] In his presence Taksin was beaten to death with a cudgel of sandalwood sewn in a sack according to the method of execution prescribed by law for members of royal families.[42]

One is taken aback by the fate of this man to whom Thailand is so deeply indebted. When confronted with this tragic occurrence, one cannot feel that reasons of state provide a valid justification for his death. At the same time it is not permissible to reckon the execution of Taksin as a personal or political stain on the character of the founder of the new dynasty.[43] Perhaps there might have been another way of keeping Taksin from affairs of state, as, for example, in the custody of a Buddhist monastery—an alternative he had already decided. But these are theoretical speculations which probably do not do justice to the facts of the case at that time.

The corpse of Taksin was at first interred at Wat Bang Yi Rŭa Tai, and later, probably in 1784,[44] was burned in the presence of Rama I and the Maha Uparat in a solemn ceremony according to Buddhist rites.[45] The proclamation of Rama I as the king of Thailand and the provisional coronation, including a procession on the Mae Nam Čau Phraya, took place on June 10, 1782.[46] One of the first deeds of the new king was the command to create a new capital city on the bank of the Mae Nam Čau Phraya located opposite Thonburi;[47] another was to elevate the rank of all members of the royal household, deserving officials and officers.[48]

[41] *Phraratcha Phongsawadan Krung Thonburi*, p. 211.

[42] *Ibid.*, footnote 38, and Chakrabongse, *op. cit.*, p. 79.

[43] As circles hostile to the dynasty attempted to do after 1932, often with arguments of rather primitive character having no foundation in fact. See the detailed references on this point in Vella, "The Impact of the West on the Government of Thailand," pp. 366 *et seq.*; Chakrabongse, *op. cit.*, p. 79, is also generally relevant to this question.

[44] In the year of the Great Dragon according to *P.P.R.I*, p. 89.

[45] *P.P.*, p. 228; Narinthewi, *op. cit.*, p. 208.

[46] Detailed descriptions are to be found in Thiphakarawong, *op. cit.*, p. 12; *P.P.*, p. 196; *Čotmaihet hon*, p. 9; Dhani Nivat, *Phraphutha Yǫt Fa songfŭnfu wathanatham*, pp. 3 *et seq.*; *Rŭang kio kap krung kau*, pp. 2 *et seq.*; Phitsanakha, *op. cit.*, pp. 35 *et seq.*

[47] See p. 17.

[48] Sommot Amǫraphan, *Song tang phra bǫrǫmawongsanuwong*, pp. 24 *et seq.*, and *Chaloem phra yot čau nai*, pp. 30 *et seq.*; Phitsanakha, *op. cit.*, pp. 37 *et seq.*; *P.P.R.I*, pp. 14 *et seq.*; *P.P.*, p. 198; also compare Čulalongkǫn, *Thamaniem ratchatrakun nai krung sayam*, pp. 1 *et seq.*

The younger brother of the king was nominated to Maha Uparat, thereby acquiring the highest rank after that of king.[49] The two elder sisters still living were accorded the rank of Somdet Phra Čau Phi Nang.[50] The children of the king[51] present at the inauguration of the new government and the children of his brothers and sisters were elevated in rank to a degree appropriate to their ancestry.[52] The king took personal interest in their careful education.[53]

Rama I formally solicited the Emperor of China to sanction his succession to the throne. Accordingly, a legation with tributes and circulars was dispatched to Peking.[54]

After the completion of the first city structures in Bangkok, particularly the royal palaces, the definitive coronation took place in accordance with traditional rites.[55] This occasioned a general public festival on a large scale.

The king called together an assembly of all members of the royal household, all courtiers, Brahmans and Buddhist scholars, who were commanded to prepare every detail of the necessary ceremonies exactly as prescribed.[56] At the expense of the royal treasury food was given to the monks, and Buddhist ceremonies took place as well as theatrical performances and dancing. Small amounts of money were distributed among the people.

When Rama I was not engaged in military campaigns, he passed the day according to a definite plan.[57] Around nine o'clock he gave the

[49] Damrong, *Song phra ǫng;* Damrong, *Tamnan wang na*, pp. 1 *et seq.;* Quaritch-Wales, *Siamese State Ceremonies*, pp. 22, 52 *et seq.* Shortly after this nomination the Maha Uparat was the object of an attempted assassination for reasons which remain unknown; see *P.P.R.I*, pp. 68 *et seq.;* Narinthewi, *op. cit.*, p. 203.

[50] "Elder royal sister."

[51] *Ratchasakunwong*, pp. 6 *et seq.*

[52] Further details in *P.P.R.I*, pp. 14 *et seq.*

[53] Information concerning the level of culture and educational methods in Thailand during the time of Rama I may be found in Damrong, *Laksana sŭksa*, pp. 117 *et seq.*

[54] Details and references in Skinner, *Chinese Society in Thailand*, p. 24, and in Fairbank and Teng, "On the Ch'ing Tributary System," p. 184; compare also the *Nirat pai mŭang čin* by Mahanuphap; note also the remark in Chapter IV, footnote 22.

[55] Quaritch-Wales, *Siamese State Ceremonies*, pp. 67 *et seq.*

[56] For a detailed description including even details of the royal vestments, see *P.P.R.I*, pp. 93–104.

[57] Dhani Nivat, *Phra Phutha Yǫt Fa songfŭnfu wathanatham*, pp. 26 *et seq.;* Dhani Nivat, "The Reconstruction of Rama I of the Chakry Dynasty," pp. 39 *et seq.; P.P.R.I*, pp. 347 *et seq.; P.P.*, pp. 465 *et seq.;* Phitsanakha, *op. cit.*, pp. 85 *et seq.;* Chakrabongse, *op. cit.*, pp. 113 *et seq.* Concerning the origin of these

monks who were passing before his palace nourishment for the day in their bowls of alms.[58] At ten o'clock he invited other monks to dine in the palace in his presence. In the morning hours immediately following there were official audiences for the highest officials and for members of the royal household. First the king heard the report of the Phra Khlang on the expenditure for the royal household and the other uses to which the government money was put. Members of his family and officers of the bodyguard were then admitted to his presence. Immediately afterwards the heads of the different departments made their reports and awaited the commands of the king.

After this audience Rama I retired to the interior of the palace where he had his breakfast. During this meal officials of the inner palace were permitted to ask for an audience concerning matters of a more private nature, and people engaged in particular tasks with which they had been charged by the king made their reports at this time. The evening meal was at six o'clock, and at seven the king was in conversation with Buddhist monks. Afterwards there were again public audiences, particularly for such ministers as the Mahatthai, the Kalahom, the Phra Khlang, the Yomarat, among others, and for the provincial governors with whom affairs of state were discussed. These audiences usually came to an end around ten o'clock in the evening, but in times of crisis they sometimes lasted until midnight.

An essential part of the affairs of state was to be found in the numerous ceremonies[59] with which the king had to concern himself for a number of different reasons. Most of these ceremonies took place in great magnificence and splendor and involved the whole apparatus of the state.[60]

With youthful members of the royal household the tonsure ceremony had to be performed.[61] The ordination of the eldest son of the

phraratchanukit see in particular Phitsanakha, *op. cit.*, and also *Phraratchanukit*, pp. 1 *et seq.*, where reference is made to the laws of Manu and, following this, to the *kot monthienban* issued under Trailokanat, from whose prescriptions about "royal duties" those of Rama I, to be sure, differ very considerably.

[58] *bat.*

[59] *Tamra krabuon sadet*, pp. 452 *et seq.*, describes more than twenty such ceremonies for a period of ten years, 1782–1792.

[60] In almost all of the Thai historical records the description of the ceremonies is of a copiousness and minuteness of detail which could scarcely be surpassed and takes up a great amount of space.

[61] Quaritch-Wales, *Siamese State Ceremonies*, p. 127; *Laksana kan phraratcha phithi sokan nai ratchakan thi nǔng*, pp. 588 *et seq.*, and pp. 593–632. We know of twenty-seven tonsure ceremonies during the period 1802–1809: *P.P.R.I*, pp. 342 *et seq.*; *P.P.*, pp. 460 *et seq.*

king was celebrated in a particularly solemn manner; he was ordained as a monk in Wat Si Ratanasasadaram together with two of the king's nephews.[62] Other members of the royal house and also officials were, in solemn ceremony, assigned to various posts of different kinds[63] or elevated in rank. In both cases special committees were set up whose task it was to examine the merits of the people in question and to report to the king.[64]

The king had new processional boats and a new throne-ship built so that the numerous processions on water could take place in a suitable manner.[65]

Several times during the reign of Rama I white elephants were brought to Bangkok from the provinces, and these events were always interpreted as good omens.[66] In a solemn ceremony each elephant was given a name.

As time went on more and more members of the royal family died. Cremation of the corpses was accompanied by a greater or lesser degree of splendor in accordance with the rank of the deceased. The deaths of the two elder sisters of Rama I, Si Sudarak and Sadawadi, occurred in September and November 1799, respectively. A new urn was specially made for each of them.[67] On the occasion of their deaths, the king of Annam sent a letter of condolence and also three *hap*[68] of honey, ten *hap* of sugar, and silk cloth as gifts.[69]

The nephew of the king, Somdet Phra Čau Lan Thoe Čau Fa Krom Luong Thepharirak,[70] died in 1805, and one year later the Krom Phraratcha Wang Lang.[71] They both had served the king as outstandingly good generals in the long wars against Burma throughout the years. The Maha Uparat died in 1803. Before his death he had very

[62] *P.P.R.I*, pp. 180 *et seq.; P.P.*, pp. 301 *et seq.*

[63] Sommot Amǫraphan, *Chaloem phra yot čau nai*, pp. 31 *et seq.;* compare *ibid.*, pp. 21 *et seq.*, the references on the origins of the nomination ceremonies; *P.P.R.I*, p. 308; *P.P.*, pp. 215, 428.

[64] Sommot Amǫraphan, *Song tang phra bǫrǫmawongsanuwong*, pp. 25 *et seq.*

[65] *P.P.R.I*, p. 344; Quaritch-Wales, *Siamese State Ceremonies*, pp. 200 *et seq.* Some of the royal boats built by Rama I still exist and are used in royal processions today.

[66] *P.P.R.I*, pp. 89, 245, 277 *et seq.*, 297, 318, 339; *P.P.*, pp. 365, 397 *et seq.*, 417, 438, 457; Narinthewi, *op. cit.*, p. 257.

[67] Narinthewi, *op. cit.*, p. 257; *Tamnan phra kot*, pp. 109, 112.

[68] One *hap* is equal to about 60 kilograms.

[69] *P.P.R.I*, p. 264.

[70] *Ibid.*, *P.P.R.I*, p. 315; *P.P.*, p. 435.

[71] *Čotmaihet hon*, pp. 12 *et seq.;* Narinthewi, *op. cit.*, p. 276; Čulalongkǫn, *Phraratchawitčan*, pp. 276 *et seq.; P.P.R.I*, pp. 327, 336 (with detailed description of the funeral ceremony); *P.P.*, pp. 446, 455.

serious dissensions with the king, his elder brother, and after his death there were similar dissensions between his sons and the king. Generally speaking, relations between the Maha Uparat and the king were almost always under a cloud and were frequently characterized by ill will and jealousy on both sides.

During the wars against the Burmese the achievements of the Maha Uparat had been outstanding, and his military services and abilities were at least equal to those of the king. It even appears that for a time his prestige as general overshadowed that of the king.[72] Nevertheless, until shortly before the death of the Maha Uparat there had been only occasional dissensions between him and the king. Rama I was repeatedly obliged to accommodate himself to the military judgment of Maha Uparat, reputed to be better than his own.[73] One incident in the year 1796 that characterizes the rivalry between them has come down to us as follows.[74]

A contest between the boat of the Main Palace, that is, the residence of the king, and the boat of the Front Palace, the residence of the Maha Uparat, had been arranged. With a view to winning the race, the Maha Uparat had secretly trained a second crew while at the same time he attempted to give a false impression of the first, weaker one. This became known to the king who thereupon cancelled the contest. This so infuriated the Maha Uparat that during the following weeks he did not appear for the daily audience.

In fact, he did not appear again until two months later, when he demanded an increase in his annuity. The 1,000 *chang*[75] of silver which he received for his household were insufficient, he alleged. Rama I replied that the financial resources of the country must first be used for the benefit of the country as a whole, and that only the remainder could be used for private purposes. If the Maha Uparat was in need of more money he should fit out some junks and engage in commerce with China, the king added. The Maha Uparat was not satisfied with this answer, however, and did not appear for another audience. In both palaces the guards were strengthened and their arms increased. Čau Phraya Ratanaphiphit learned that preparations for an uprising were

[72] Compare, for example, the behavior of the Phra Čau Kawila of Chiengmai in 1802, see p. 91.

[73] For example, before the battle of Lat Ya, see p. 53, and after the unsuccessful attack on Thavoi in 1787, see p. 78.

[74] *P.P.R.I*, pp. 255 *et seq.*; *P.P.*, pp. 375 *et seq.*

[75] One *chang* is equal to 604.53 grams.

being made in the Front Palace and informed the king accordingly. The main palace was then surrounded by a thick cordon of troops, and there was a real danger of serious conflict.[76] However, the two elder sisters were finally able to bring about a reconciliation.

In 1803 the Maha Uparat returned to Bangkok from the last Burmese war[77] earlier than expected.[78] His illness was steadily growing worse, and there was no longer any prospect of recovery. The King himself hastened to the sickbed of his brother.[79] However, when he and his retinue were surrounding the resting-place of the Maha Uparat, the latters' employees approached in such a hostile manner that the king was obliged to take precautions for his own security. On Thursday, the fourth day of the waning moon in the twelfth lunar month 2346 (1803),[80] the Maha Uparat died in his throne room Buraphaphimuk in his sixty-first year after a life filled with struggle. The king and all members of the royal household said their prayers at the deathbed. A new urn was made for the deceased[81] at the command of Rama I.

The Maha Uparat had rendered great services to his country, both for its military liberation and for its political restoration.[82] He had also distinguished himself as the builder of fortifications at Bangkok, of numerous palaces and temples,[83] and as a poet[84] and zealous promoter of Buddhism.[85] He had fourteen sons and twenty-three daughters from thirty-three women.[86]

On the occasion of the solemn cremation of the Maha Uparat, the king of Annam sent a delegation with a personal letter and numerous gifts, including five pieces[87] of gold, fifty pieces of silver, 100 bales of

[76] *P.P.R.I*, p. 256.

[77] See p. 87.

[78] *P.P.R.I*, p. 298; *P.P.*, p. 418.

[79] Narinthewi, *op. cit.*, p. 265; *P.P.R.I*, p. 299; Damrong, *Tamnan wang na*, p. 32, doubts this, and the doubt is probably justified with regard to the assertion that Rama I himself spent six days caring for the sick Maha Uparat.

[80] *Čotmaihet hon*, p. 12.

[81] *Tamnan phra kot*, pp. 109, 112 *et seq.*; *P.P.R.I*, p. 300.

[82] As is obvious from later chapters of this work. See also Wanarat, *Thetsana*, pp. 132 *et seq.*; Sonakun, *Prawatsat Thai samai krung ratanakosin yuk raek*, p. 13; *P.P.R.I*, p. 300.

[83] Enumerated in *P.P.R.I*, pp. 301–305, and in *P.P.*, pp. 422–425.

[84] Mahasurasinghanat, *Phra bǫwǫn ratc̦ha prawat lae phra bǫwǫn ratcha niphon*, pp. 10, 17.

[85] *P.P.R.I*, pp. 68 *et seq.*, 183 *et seq.*

[86] *Phra nam orot thida*, pp. 154 *et seq.*; *ibid.*, note 84, pp. 3 *et seq.*; *Ratchasakunwong*, pp. 94 *et seq.*; Sonakun, *op. cit.*, pp. 7 *et seq.*

[87] *Lim*, "lump," the weight of which is unknown to the author.

silk of different colors, five *hap*[88] of sugar-candy, thirty *hap* of sugar, 100 pieces of white cloth, and five *hap* of honey.[89] In his covering letter, Gia Long urged the king to nominate his eldest son as new Maha Uparat without further delay in order to secure continuity in the succession to the throne and peace in the country.[90]

Yet before the cremation took place, plans for a new uprising originating in the Front Palace became known. All appearances indicated that before his death the Maha Uparat himself spread the idea that it was only because of his efforts and plans that the throne of Thailand had become so powerful.[91] He had himself carried into his throne hall where he broke out into complaints and lamentations. He had hoped to be able to enjoy for a long time the rich booty he had brought back from the wars, but this would now belong to someone else, he complained.

One day as his illness grew worse, he had himself carried once again into the Wat Mahathat where he consecrated his sword to the temple in connection with the making of a candle-holder. He then attempted to kill himself with his sword. On the way back to the Front Palace, the Maha Uparat, together with his sons Lamduon and Inthapat, made continual inflammatory speeches, saying that things would go badly for his sons and his retinue after his death and that they would not receive any part of his property as all of it would go to the Main Palace.

Lamduon, Inthapat and others then formed a conspiracy against Rama I. Their plans, however, did not remain secret and became known to the king. Immediately after the death of the Maha Uparat, Lamduon and Inthapat were arrested. They admitted that on the day of the cremation of their father they had planned an uprising, and they also betrayed the names of their fellow conspirators. All the guilty, including the sons of the Maha Uparat, were beheaded.[92]

Because of this occurrence the king at first refused to take part in the ceremony of his brother's cremation. However, his advisers convinced him that it would be better for him to take part in it, for

[88] See footnote 68 of this chapter.

[89] Return presents from Rama I included arms, diamond rings, a diadem, earrings, loose precious stones, bedspreads brocaded in gold, in addition to further presents from the eldest son of the king. See *P.P.R.I*, p. 313.

[90] *Ibid.*, Thiphakarawong, *op. cit.*, p. 312; *P.P.*, p. 432.

[91] *P.P.R.I*, pp. 305 *et seq.; P.P.*, pp. 425 *et seq.;* Chakrabongse, *op. cit.*, p. 111.

[92] *Čotmaihet hon*, p. 12; Narinthewi, *op. cit.*, p. 268; Čulalongkǫn, *Phraratchawitčan*, pp. 268 *et seq.; P.P.R.I*, p. 308.

otherwise many people who knew nothing of the planned uprising would learn about it if the king should not be present.[93]

It was not until 1806,[94] three years after the death of the Maha Uparat, that the eldest son of the king, Somdet Phra Čau Luk Thoe Čau Fa Krom Luong Isarasunthǫn, in a solemn ceremony[95] in the throne hall Dusit Mahaprasat, was nominated as the new Maha Uparat.[96] This event was made the occasion for a public festival lasting many days. However, the new Maha Uparat did not immediately take up residence in the Front Palace, for the descendants of his predecessor were still living there. Accordingly, he continued to live in his former palace, the old one of Taksin. The king of Annam "greeted with joy" the nomination of the new Maha Uparat,[97] whose first official deed was the establishment of a large court.[98]

The last years of the reign of Rama I did not bring with them any important events of a warlike nature. Therefore, the king was able to dedicate himself to the administration of his country and to fine arts. His court once again became the center of the most important literary figures of the country. Important works of Thai poetry[99] and history[100] date from this period, some of them composed by the king himself.[101]

The king's strength gradually diminished with his increasing age. When there was an audience, he had himself carried on a stretcher. Immediately after the consecration of the Wat Si Sasadaram[102] he became seriously ill and gave all his possessions to the Maha Uparat, successor to the throne. On Thursday, the nineteenth day of the waning moon in the ninth lunar month[103] 2352 (1809), Rama I passed away in his throne hall around midnight.[104] The first king of the Čakri dynasty

[93] *P.P.R.I*, p. 311.

[94] Concerning the exact date we have conflicting statements, see *Čotmaihet hon*, p. 12, and *P.P.R.I*, p. 329.

[95] *Phraratcha phithi uparatchaphisek.*

[96] Narinthewi, *op. cit.*, p. 281; detailed description of the ceremony in Čulalongkǫn, *Phraratchawitčan*, pp. 281–288; *P.P.R.I*, pp. 329 *et seq.*

[97] *P.P.R.I*, pp. 337 *et seq.*; *P.P.*, pp. 455 *et seq.*

[98] On this matter see the full account in Sommot Amǫraphan, *Song tang phra bǫrǫmawongsanuwong*, pp. 28 *et seq.*, 57 *et seq.*

[99] Including parts of the *Ramakien*, *Inau*, *Unarut*, *Ratchathirat*, *Nirat* poems of Sunthǫn Phu, and the translation of the Chinese history *Saihan.*

[100] Including the *Phongsawadan chabap Phančanthanumat.*

[101] On the literary work of Rama I see particularly Dhani Nivat, *Phra Phutha Yǫt Fa songfůnfu wathanatham*, pp. 52–93; Dhani Nivat, "The Ramakien," p. 35.

[102] Narinthewi, *op. cit.*, p. 299; Čulalongkǫn, *Phraratchawitčan*, pp. 300 *et seq.*

[103] *I.e.*, September 7.

[104] Statements about the moment of the king's death are not the same in all accounts: *Čotmaihet hon*, p. 13, "midnight"; *P.P.R.I*, p. 352, "sam yam," in other

had lived beyond the age of seventy.[105] He had ruled over Thailand for twenty-seven years of his life. In the *Recollections of Narinthewi*, the younger sister of the king, the remark is to be found[106] that the kings of the Čakri dynasty would succeed one another for a period of 150 years.[107] This prophecy was not fulfilled, but the absolute rule of the Čakri dynasty did indeed come to an end exactly in the year 1932, 150 years after Rama I's accession to the throne.

Rama I had 42 children,[108] of whom seventeen were sons and twenty-five were daughters.[109] While he was still alive the king had had an urn made for himself.[110] The solemn ceremony of cremation took place under his son and successor, Rama II.[111]

---

words around 3:42 A.M.; *idem. P.P.*, p. 470; Narinthewi, *op. cit.*, p. 326, "phlau yam."

[105] Corresponding to the conflicting statements about the year of Rama I's birth (see footnotes 9 and 10 of this chapter), his age at the time of his death is also variously given. See Chakrabongse, *op. cit.*, p. 114, and *P.P.R.I*, p. 353.

[106] Narinthewi, *op. cit.*, p. 220; but according to Čulalongkọn, *Phraratchawitčan*, pp. 220 *et seq.*, this is to be doubted though the reasons for these doubts are not convincing.

[107] According to Chakrabongse, *op. cit.*, p. 116, this prophecy was made by the king himself. That is probably a mistake and, in my opinion, relates to the above-mentioned passage in Narinthewi, *op. cit.*

[108] *Ratchasakunwong*, pp. 6 *et seq.*, gives detailed information about the dates for the children of Rama I; Sonakun, *op. cit.*, pp. 7 *et seq.*

[109] Two daughters of Rama I, Čau Montha and Čau Ubon, became known as poetesses; from the latter the *Kuman kham chan* has been published (Bangkok, 1917).

[110] *Tamnan phra kot*, p. 113; Narinthewi, *op. cit.*, p. 267.

[111] For details of the ceremony see Damrong, *Ratchakan thi sọng*, vol. 1, pp. 1 *et seq.*

Chapter II

THE FOUNDATION OF BANGKOK

BANGKOK WAS FOUNDED at the very beginning of the new dynasty. In 1782, the year of his ascension to the throne, Rama I gave the command[1] to build a new capital city on the eastern side of the Mae Nam Čau Phraya opposite the residence of Taksin.

The residence of Taksin, probably a temporary structure, was located by the Khlǫng Bangkok Yai next to two highly frequented wats, Wat Čaeng and Wat Tha, both hemmed in by markets.[2] This locality was therefore deemed unsuitable for a royal residence of representative character. Nevertheless, military considerations appear to have been decisive in the choice of its location.[3]

Thonburi lay on the western side of the Mae Nam Čau Phraya and was therefore directly exposed to a Burmese attack by land. On the other hand, the eastern bank was semicircular in shape, bordering a great bend in the river which enclosed this territory from the west and the south. The northern and eastern sides could be barred easily by a canal. This territory was therefore considerably easier to defend than Thonburi on the western side. A city located on both sides of the river with the Mae Nam Čau Phraya flowing through the center of it did not seem advantageous to the king for strategic reasons. During the reign of Taksin, Rama I had taken part in the defense of Phitsanulok,[4] which was also divided into two parts by a river, even though the river was not as deep and broad. He therefore knew how difficult it was during wartime to move troops from one part of the city to another because of lack of bridges. The idea of including Thonburi in the plan for the new city was therefore abandoned.

[1] Narinthewi, *op. cit.*, p. 184; Sonakun, *op. cit.*, pp. 1 *et seq.;* see in particular *ibid.*, pp. 15 *et seq.;* see also *Somphot phra nakhǫn khrop rǫi pi*, pp. 1 *et seq.*
[2] Damrong, *Thai rop Phama*, vol. 2, p. 164.
[3] *P.P.R.I*, pp. 11 *et seq.*
[4] See p. 4.

The territory opposite to Thonburi was at that time an extensive swamp. However, since it was not flooded continuously, it was possible to drain the land, and plans to this effect may already have been made during the time of Taksin.[5] Therefore, after the necessary drainage operations, the building of the royal palace was begun.[6] The headmen of the Department of Craftsmen and Domestic Servants,[7] Phraya Thammathikon and Phraya Wičitnawi, were charged with this task. The place which had been chosen for the palace was occupied by a rich Chinese merchant upon whom the rank of Phraya had been conferred. This proprietor, together with the surrounding Chinese community,[8] were asked to transfer their residence to the "gardens," that is to say, to territory which had not yet been inhabited, beyond the future heart of the city.[9] A new Chinese community then arose in the region of present-day Sampheng.

The work of building the palace began at a time astrologically determined.[10] The foundation was erected on piles, and, in order to make more rapid progress, the entire structure was built of wood and enclosed within wooden palisades.[11] The layout, with its great halls, rooms and places of worship, was planned to correspond exactly to that of the old palace of Ayuthaya.[12] At the same time the palaces of the

[5] This is a conjecture on the part of Damrong, *Thai rop Phama*, vol. 2, p. 167, the truth of which cannot be definitely established but which nevertheless deserves to be treated seriously in view of the fact that the building of Bangkok began immediately after the accession o the throne of Rama I. This means that plans must have been made with regard to the difficult water situation.

[6] *Čotmaihet hon*, p. 9; *P.P.R.I*, p. 12.

[7] *Kǫng khum chang lae phai.*

[8] Concerning the origins of Bangkok we have no further information beyond this. According to Smith, *A Physician at the Court of Siam*, p. 13, the name of Bangkok means "village of the wild plum" (*Spondias pinnata*, Kurz). *Bang* signifies a "village in the lowlands." This explanation is accepted by Chakrabongse, *op. cit.*, p. 80. In Hutchinson, "Four French State Manuscripts," p. 2, a certain place, "Bangkoc," is several times mentioned, and according to a map of M. de la Mare it is located at the Mae Nam Čau Phraya, approximately the location of the present-day Bangkok. See also the map in Hutchinson, "The French Garrison at Bangkok," pp. 2, 119 *et seq.* However, further research will be necessary before "Bangkoc" can be identified with Bangkok.

[9] *P.P.R.I*, p. 12, and Damrong, *Tamnan wang kau*, p. 7. Of the "adequate compensation" mentioned in Chakrabongse, *op. cit.*, p. 80, there is no record in Thai sources.

[10] *Čotmaihet hon*, p. 9; *P.P.R.I*, p. 12.

[11] Damrong, *Tamnan wang kau*, pp. 2 *et seq.*

[12] Further details may be found in Damrong, *Tamnan wang kau*, pp. 7 *et seq.;* Damrong, *Tamnan wang na*, pp. 17 *et seq.;* Phothiprasat, *Sathapatayakam*, pp. 118 *et seq.*

Maha Uparat, the *Wang Na*,[13] and those of eight other dignitaries were built, including that of Krom Phraratcha, the *Wang Lang*.[14] In the course of the next two years twenty-six additional residences for the nobility were erected in Bangkok.[15] Except for minor variations arising from the idiosyncracies of terrain in Bangkok, all layouts followed the example of the old capital city.[16] In July, two months after the beginning of construction work, both the *Wang Luong* and the *Wang Na* were officially opened. However, further construction work went on for several years, reaching at least a provisional end in 1785.[17] As soon as the first wooden buildings were habitable, bricks were procured from the remains of Ayuthaya and used for further building, particularly for the construction of fortifications.[18] Even the fortifications of Thonburi were destroyed so that the bricks could be used for the building of Bangkok.[19]

In 1786 the king designated the city by the name which it still has today:[20] "City of the Gods, Sublime City, most precious of all the gems of Indra. . . ."

For purposes of defense and drainage, canals were made around and through the new city. Ten thousand Cambodians were forced to labor[21] on this. Beginning at Bang Lam Phu, a canal was dug to the east and to the north which delimited the boundary of the city to the east. The length of this canal, Khlǫng Rǫp Krung,[22] was around 3,426

[13] *Phraratcha wang bǫwǫn sathan mongkhon*. A detailed description of this is to be found in Damrong, *Tamnan wang na*, pp. 2 *et seq.*, and in Phothiprasat, *op. cit.*, pp. 125 *et seq.* The distinction between *Wang Luong* and *Wang Na* and the standing which this involved were retained up until the time of Rama IV. The *Wang Luong* was called *bǫrǫm*, and the *Wang Na*, *bǫwǫn*. See on this point the historical references in Damrong, *Tamnan wang na*, pp. 1 *et seq.*; see also Dhani Nivat, *The Royal Palaces*, pp. 28 *et seq.*

[14] Phothiprasat, *op. cit.*, pp. 131 *et seq.*; at the end of the reign of Rama I the *Wang Lang* was divided up into four complexes, see Damrong, *Tamnan wang kau*, p. 13.

[15] For enumeration and detailed description see Damrong, *Tamnan wang kau*, pp. 14 *et seq.*

[16] *P.P.R.I*, p. 12; Damrong, *Tamnan wang na*, pp. 17 *et seq.*; see also the references cited in footnote 29 of this chapter.

[17] *P.P.R.I*, pp. 76, 79; *P.P.*, p. 228. A detailed description of the present condition may be found in Dhani Nivat, *The Royal Palaces*, pp. 6 *et seq.*

[18] *P.P.R.I*, p. 74; Damrong, *Tamnan wang na*, p. 19; Damrong, *Thai rop Phama*, vol. 2, p. 166.

[19] *P.P.R.I*, p. 74.

[20] Complete text in *P.P.R.I*, p. 105, containing reference to the changing of the name by Mongkut, Rama IV.

[21] *Ken;* see *P.P.R.I*, p. 74; Chakrabongse, *op. cit.*, p. 98.

[22] "Canal around the city."

meters; it had a width of about 20 meters and a depth of about 2.50 meters.[23] Another large canal, Khlǫng Mahanak, was dug from the Khlǫng Rǫp Krung through the city to the Mae Nam Čau Phraya. This canal was intended primarily for the pleasure of the court and the population.

After the completion of the canal system, 5,000 Lao from Vientiane were summoned[24] to construct fortifications and walls around Bangkok. The walls were furnished with towers separated from each other by a distance of 400 meters. All officials of Bangkok and the provinces were enjoined to assist in this undertaking. The king and the Maha Uparat personally supervised the work in progress.

Rama I at first intended to put a bridge over the Khlǫng Rǫp Krung to the south of the mouth of the Khlǫng Mahanak in order to create easy access to the city for his elephants. This plan, however, was abandoned after the king had been made to understand that such a bridge would be dangerous in case of a hostile attack.[25] Furthermore, such a bridge would have interfered with navigation. A special pier was then put up at the Khlǫng Rǫp Krung to enable the elephants to cross the canal.

In the following years the fortifications and walls of Bangkok were constantly enlarged and strengthened.[26] Probably because of a rumor spread by the Burmese in 1797, to the effect that a British attack up the Mae Nam Čau Phraya was imminent,[27] Samut Prakan was also fortified as a protection against possible invasion from the sea.[28]

Construction of new temple layouts was begun at the same time as the building of the royal residence. Here, too, the example of Ayuthaya decided the architecture of the new layouts. The resemblance of the temples of Bangkok to those of Ayuthaya can be shown in detail;[29] even old names were adopted.

The Wat Phra Kaeo, Wat Si Ratanasasadaram,[30] famous as the

[23] These figures are given in *P.P.R.I*, p. 74.

[24] On this matter see Narinthewi, *op. cit.*, p. 208, and Čulalongkǫn, *Phraratchawitčan*, p. 208.

[25] *P.P.R.I*, p. 233.

[26] Narinthewi, *op. cit.*, p. 257; *P.P.*, pp. 231 *et seq.*

[27] See p. 82.

[28] *P.P.*, p. 296.

[29] Phothiprasat, *op. cit.*, pp. 132 *et seq.;* Damrong, *Munlahet haeng kan sang wat nai prathet Thai*, pp. 23 *et seq.*, gives further details about the kinds of Thai temples—*wat phutthačedi* and *wat anusawari*—and their nomenclature; *P.P.R.I*, pp. 346 *et seq.; P.P.*, pp. 464 *et seq.;* see also Döhring, *Buddhistische Tempelanlagen in Siam*, vol. I, pp. 33 *et seq.*, vols. II, III.

[30] *P.P.R.I*, pp. 80 *et seq.* For further details about the Jade Buddha, particularly

temple of the "Jade Buddha," was constructed within the royal palace. In this temple the Tripiṭaka was kept in a hall especially constructed for that purpose.

Construction work on Wat Phra Chetuphon, Wat Pho, began in 1789.[31] However, the land chosen was still swampy and full of pools and ditches.[32] Rama I therefore put 20,000 laborers to work to drain the land and built it up to a higher level. Earth was procured to the amount of 250 *chang* silver and 15 *tamlung*,[33] a tremendous task in view of the means of transportation at that time. The work on this building lasted more than twelve years, but the Ubosot was already dedicated by the king in 1791 and received the name Phra Si Sanphet. With a solemn procession the entire temple was consecrated in April, 1801,[34] and given the name Wat Phra Chetuphon. This temple may be considered one of the most significant monuments for the history of art in Bangkok. Not the least of its claims to fame are the inscriptions for which Rama I and the following kings are responsible, particularly those in the Wihan.[35]

Among the many temples which were built under Rama I, Wat Suthat is also worthy of mention because of its great artistic value. A famous statue of Buddha brought from Sukhothai was set up in this temple. In 1809, the year of the king's death, Wat Si Ratanasasadaram was consecrated with great pomp.[36] Wat Mahathat was one of the many important temples[37] built by the Maha Uparat.

---

with regard to its history: Notton, *The Chronicle of the Emerald Buddha*, pp. 3 *et seq.*; Dhani Nivat, *The Royal Palaces*, pp. 17, 20 *et seq.*; Coedès, *Les collections archéologiques du Musée National de Bangkok*, p. 33, plate XXXV; Lingat, "Le Culte du Bouddha d'Émeraude," pp. 9 *et seq.*

[31] Narinthewi, *op. cit.*, p. 187; Čulalongkǫn, *Phraratchawitčan*, pp. 187 *et seq.*; *P.P.R.I*, pp. 266 *et seq.*; *P.P.*, pp. 385 *et seq.*; *Prachum čarŭk Wat Phra Chetuphon*, pp. 1 *et seq.*

[32] A detailed description of its condition before the beginning of construction work is given in Čulalongkǫn, *Phraratchawitčan*, pp. 187 *et seq.*

[33] One *chang* is equal to 604.53 grams. One *tamlŭng* weighs about 60 grams.

[34] Detailed description in *P.P.R.I*, pp. 267 *et seq.*, and in *Prachum čarŭk Wat Phra Chetuphon, loc. cit.*, detailed information about the building itself.

[35] Collected in *Prachum čarŭk Wat Phra Chetuphon*, vols. 1, 2; see also Čulalongkǫn, *Phraratchawitčan*, pp. 187 *et seq.*, and Dhani Nivat, "The Inscriptions of Vat Jetubhon," pp. 2, 143 *et seq.* *Wihan* denotes one of the main buildings of a Thai temple for preaching, meditation and prayer.

[36] Narinthewi, *op. cit.*, pp. 299, 316; Damrong, *Munlahet haeng kan sang wat nai prathet Thai*, p. 24; *Čulalongkǫn*, *Phraratchawitčan*, pp. 317 *et seq.* Yet certain parts of this great temple appear to have been used previously, as in 2331 a report was made of a fire which was caused by carelessness and destroyed a part of the temple, *P.P.R.I*, p. 261; *P.P.*, p. 381.

[37] They are listed in *P.P.R.I*, pp. 301 *et seq.*, and in *P.P.*, pp. 422 *et seq.*

However, the construction of the city did not proceed entirely undisturbed. Because of the continuing attacks by the Burmese armies and the preparations for war made necessary by these attacks, work often came to a standstill. Moreover, fires and floods frequently destroyed the work which just had been done. During a thunderstorm in 1789 a stroke of lightning caused the portico of the throne hall to go up in flames.[38] The fire quickly spread throughout the palace. With the active assistance of the king and the Maha Uparat, it was possible to save the throne and the royal insignia.[39] And the priests succeeded in convincing Rama I that his fears that the stroke of lightning was a bad omen were not justified.[40] Construction work on a new, but somewhat smaller, throne hall was begun immediately after the fire. The example of the former throne hall, Suriyamarin in Ayuthaya, was followed in detail, and the new hall was given the name Phra Thi Nang Dusit Mahaprasat.

The chronicler records a conflagration in Sampheng during the year 1800 which extended to the Talat Nọi,[41] and in 1801 another conflagration was caused by the carelessness of some young monks.[42]

[38] The date of the fire has been recorded in terms of an astrological calendar: the first day of the crescent moon in the seventh lunar month at thirty-six minutes past midnight.

[39] *P.P.R.I*, pp. 197 *et seq.; P.P.*, pp. 317 *et seq.*

[40] *P.P.R.I*, p. 199.

[41] *Ibid.*, p. 265; *P.P.*, p. 385.

[42] *P.P.R.I*, p. 281; *P.P.*, p. 401.

Chapter III

INTERNAL RESTORATION

1. The Administration of the Kingdom

The king and the government

The position of the king, Rama I, conformed to the previous tradition of the Phra Thammasat. The omnipotence of the governmental power of the Thai kings,[1] limited only by the religious prescriptions of this law, was taken over without modification by the first ruler of the new dynasty. During his twenty-seven year reign, Rama I appears to have concentrated all governmental power in his own person without controversy.

The traditional arrangement of the highest administrative position was in the same way in its fundamental principles taken over from the Ayuthaya period, exactly as maintained by the kings of the last Ayuthaya dynasty.[2] The separate regional ministries were maintained in accordance with the means of transportation and communication prevailing at that time.

At the same time, however, there were also supreme offices having authority over special fields, in particular for commerce, economy and justice, for the administration of the royal court, and for matters concerning the Buddhist religion.[3] However, after 1782 a number of

[1] On this point see particularly Dhani Nivat, "The Old Siamese Conception of the Monarchy," pp. 2, 94 *et seq.*; Phraya Nitisatphaisan, *Prawatsat kotmai Thai*, pp. 87 *et seq.*

[2] The fundamentals are described in Quaritch-Wales, *Ancient Siamese Government and Administration*, pp. 69 *et seq.*

[3] Detailed information in *ibid.*, pp. 92 *et seq.*, and in Damrong, *Laksana kan pokkhrǫng prathet sayam tae boran*, pp. 1 *et seq.*; Damrong-Ratchasena, *Thetsaphiban*, pp. 1 *et seq.* (both of these works are written from a historical point of view); Čulalongkǫn, *Phraratcha damrat kaekhai kan pokkhrǫng*, pp. 1 *et seq.*, a very informative piece of work; Phadung Khwaen Pračan, *Latthitamaniem ratsadǫn phak Isan*, pp. 25 *et seq.*, goes into particular detail about northern and eastern Thailand.

changes were made in the division of the areas of authority of the various ministries, changes sometimes made for personal reasons and sometimes conditioned by objective, matter-of-fact considerations. These were:

1. The office of the *Mahatthai*, which administered the regional ministry for North Thailand, remained unchanged. Čau Phraya Ratanaphiphit (Son), who came from the hierarchy of officials of the Thonburi epoch, became the first *Mahatthai* under Rama I with the rank of *Samuhanayok*.[4]
2. Toward the end of the Ayuthaya epoch, those provinces which were normally administered by the ministry for South Thailand, the *Krom Kalahom*, had been put partly under the control of the *Krom Mahatthai* and partly under the control of the *Krom Tha*, owing to the fact that the Kalahom of that time had been guilty of mistakes having serious practical consequences.[5] The present Kalahom, Čau Phraya Mahasena,[6] (Pli), who had been governor of Petchabun under Taksin and had distinguished himself by particular bravery in the course of the restoration struggles, was highly favored by the new king.[7] The provinces under the *Krom Mahatthai* and *Krom Tha* were therefore now taken away from these ministries and again placed under the control of the *Krom Kalahom*. Nineteen districts[8] previously placed under the *Krom Tha* and one which had been under the *Krom Mahatthai* were involved in this reorganization. They were as follows: Songkhla, Pathalung, Nakhọn Si Thammarat, Chaiya, Langsuon, Chumphọn, Pathiwa, Khlọngwan, Kui, Pran, Tanausi, Marit, Kra, Takuapa, Takuathung, Phangnga, Thalang, Kančanaburi, Saiyok[9] and Phetburi, the one province taken from the *Krom Mahatthai*.

[4] Dhani Nivat, "The Reconstruction of Rama I of the Chakry Dynasty," p. 43; *Senabọdi mahatthai lae nakhọnban*, p. 1; on titles in general see Quaritch-Wales, *Ancient Siamese Government and Administration*, p. 85, and also the literature mentioned in footnote 21 of Chapter I. For meaning of *Samuhanayok* see footnote 22 of Chapter I.

[5] *P.P.R.I*, p. 24; Sommot Amọraphan, *Song tang phra bọrọmawongsanuwong*, p. 25.

[6] Title of the highest official—*senabọdi*—of the *Krom Kalahom.*

[7] *P.P.R.I*, p. 24.

[8] In the Thai sources recorded as *mŭang*.

[9] The old provincial names are here kept, but today some of these are obsolete.

However, Čau Phraya Mahasena was killed in action during the second attack of the Thai on Thavoi in 1793.[10] First the Phraya Phonlathep (Pin) and then the Phraya Yomarat Bunak were nominated as his successors.[11]

3. After its southern provinces had been detached, the *Krom Tha*, the "harbor authority" under the *Phra Khlang*, had the administration of only eight districts, most of which were either on the coast or very close to it. These were Nonthaburi, Samut Prakan, Sakhǫnburi, Chonburi, Banglamung, Rayong, Čanthaburi and Trat; moreover, Samut Songkhram, which had previously belonged to the *Krom Mahatthai*, was now attached to the *Krom Tha*, while, on the other hand, Chachoensau, previously under the *Krom Tha*, was now handed over to the *Krom Mahatthai*.[12] Consequently, the activity of the *Phra Khlang* was once again essentially limited to the administration of finances and the commercial relations of the kingdom.[13]

   The first *Phra Khlang* under Rama I was Phiphathanakosa, who had previously been in the service of Taksin. He was later alleged to be mentally ill[14] and was relieved of his position. Nevertheless, he was able to continue work in the *Krom Tha* with the title Phraya Si Akarat. He was succeeded by Luong Sǫrawichit, who had already proved very satisfactory as customs officer and at that time was one of the most well-known poets at the court of Rama I.[15] After his death in 1805,[16] the office of the *Phra Khlang* was taken over by Phraya Si Phiphat, who rose to the position of *Samuhanayok* under Rama II.

4. The office of the *Phraya Yomarat*, in charge of the *Krom Mŭang*,[17] was taken over by Luong Intharathibǫdisiharat Rǫng Mŭang after the coronation of Rama I. He had particularly distinguished himself in the campaigns of the epoch

[10] See p. 79.

[11] Dhani Nivat, "The Reconstruction of Rama I of the Chakry Dynasty," pp. 43 *et seq.*; *P.P.R.I*, p. 359; *P.P.*, p. 478.

[12] *P.P.R.I*, p. 24.

[13] On the changing development of the *Krom Tha* see Quaritch-Wales, *Ancient Siamese Government and Administration*, pp. 90 *et seq.*

[14] *P.P.R.I*, pp. 213, 359; *P.P.*, p. 479.

[15] *Prawat wannakhadi Thai*, pp. 301 *et seq.*; Dhani Nivat, "The Reconstruction of Rama I of the Chakry Dynasty," p. 43.

[16] *Prawat wannakhadi Thai*, p. 302.

[17] Approximately "office for district administration."

of Taksin; however, in the first Burmese war under Rama I he did not properly discharge his duties as general and was relieved of his position.[18] His successors were the later Phraya Kalahom Bunak[19] and the stepbrother of the latter, Bunma.[20]

The Krom Mŭang, also under Rama I, was above all responsible for the internal security and safety of the capital, which means that this office had police and judicial functions.[21]

5. Čau Phraya Thammathibǫdi, the *senabǫdi* of the *Krom Wang*,[22] was at first Bunrot. However, together with the Phraya Yomarat Luong Intharathibǫdi, he was not a satisfactory officer at Ratburi in 1785 and was relieved of his position. Various courtiers of Rama I succeeded him.[23]

   The *Krom Wang* was responsible for all matters directly connected with the court, and therefore for the preparations of the ceremonies which were of supreme importance in Thailand at that time. In addition, the Čau Phraya Thammathibǫdi was responsible for the nomination of certain judicial and administrative officials in the kingdom.[24]
6. *Phraya Phonlathep*,[25] who administered the *Krom Na*,[26] was at first the later Kalahom (Pin) and after him the Čau Phraya Phonlathep Bunak. The *Krom Na* was responsible for the supply of rice and for the provision of other agricultural products for the government storehouses.[27]

In addition to these six principal ministries, the heads of which might well be described as constituting the "cabinet," there were numerous other offices in the central administration.[28]

[18] See p. 55.
[19] See above under 2., this chapter.
[20] *P.P.R.I*, p. 360; *P.P.*, p. 480.
[21] *Yomarat*, "judge of the hell."
[22] "Office (for the administration) of the palace."
[23] *P.P.R.I*, p. 261; *P.P.*, p. 481.
[24] See Quaritch-Wales, *Ancient Siamese Government and Administration*, pp. 92 *et seq.*
[25] A title probably derived from *Phalathep*, the name of the elder brother of Krishna.
[26] "Office for the administration of arable land."
[27] Quaritch-Wales, *Ancient Siamese Government and Administration*, p. 89.
[28] *P.P.R.I*, pp. 18 *et seq.*, pp. 26 *et seq.*

The administration of the provinces

The tendency to centralize the administration as much as possible continued under Rama I. This was particularly necessary with regard to the outer provinces, which after 1767 had become more or less independent.

The division into four classes of provinces, taken over from the past, was maintained.[29] All provincial governors were appointed from Bangkok either on the basis of merit or in accordance with the wishes of Bangkok, and it was from there that they were recalled.[30] An advisory committee consisting of judges and high Buddhist priests assisted the king in this task. Members of the committee made out lists enumerating the merits and services of those to be promoted and with appropriate suggestions regarding promotion.[31] The fact that the emphasis in this matter was placed almost entirely on military qualifications is easy enough to understand, for the country was constantly threatened with new Burmese attacks.[32]

Immediately after the accession of Rama I to the throne, twenty-one new appointments were made to the office of governor in the provinces.[33] It appears, however, that in the choice of governors for those provinces which formerly had been more or less independent preference was given to resident noble families and to the succession from the father to the son. This was particularly true of the northern Lao provinces and for the southernmost provinces, which formerly had been Malayan principalities or, as in the case of Nakhǫn Si Thammarat, the capital of a great realm. As compensation, the sons of these governors came to the court at Bangkok as pages; this was, to be sure, an honor for the pages and a stage toward their later careers; however, at the same time it gave security to the kings of Thailand with regard to the loyalty of the governors.[34] The governor of Nakhǫn Si Thammarat, who under Taksin had been made a "prince of the country,"[35]

[29] Quaritch-Wales, *Ancient Siamese Government and Administration*, pp. 109 *et seq.*

[30] See, for example, *P.P.R.I*, p. 90, among others.

[31] Sommot Amǫraphan, *Song tang phra bǫrǫmawongsanuwong*, pp. 25 *et seq.*

[32] Compare Damrong, *Tamnan kan thi Thai rien phasa angkrit*, p. 111, "under Rama I only the man who had distinguished himself in war was respected."

[33] *P.P.R.I*, p. 23 f. On elevation in rank see also Sommot Amǫraphan, *Tang čau phraya*, pp. 1 *et seq.*, pp. 9 *et seq.*

[34] See, for example, Kathathǫnthǫranin, *Phongsawadan Phratabǫng*, p. 4, among others.

[35] *Čau prathetsarat.*

was now deprived of this title. At his request, however, his son-in-law, Čau Phat, was appointed governor in his place, although he was given a lower title.[36] At the same time Songkhla was detached and raised to the status of a separate province having the rank of a *mŭang tri.*[37]

In the borderlands, which as a result of military measures came under the supreme authority of Bangkok, there gradually arose new semi-independent dominions. These, to be sure, were not officially under the jurisdiction of the central authority in Bangkok but were nevertheless dependent to the extent that their rulers could continue in power only if this was agreeable to the Bangkok authorities.[38]

A detailed account[39] has come down to us concerning the hierarchy of one province, Phathalung, during the time of Rama I. It gives us insight into the fine-meshed net of Thai administration at that time.

At the head of the province stood the governor, the *čau mŭang*, who had the title of a Phraya.[40] He was the absolute master of all executive power and jurisdiction in his district. He was at the same time commander of the military forces stationed in the province, though the governor of Phathalung was subject to the governor of Nakhǫn Si Thammarat in case of military affairs. The realm of his authority was so great that even a verdict of life or death lay in his hands. On the other hand, the higher officials[41] of his province were appointed from Bangkok, usually by a deputy of the king or by the king himself. They were as follows:

1. The *Phra Palat*, the deputy governor.
2. The *Luong Yokrabat*, who had approximately the function of public prosecutor.
3. From one to three *Luong Phu Chui*, who were charged with various administrative duties and had titles corresponding to their activities.[42]
4. The *Phra Phon Čang Wen Dan*, who was the highest customs officer of the province.

[36] *P.P.R.I*, p. 91.

[37] See the information in footnotes 386 and 388 of Chapter IV.

[38] This was particularly true of Lao territories; see for example Amǫrawǫngwičit, *Phongsawadan Isan*, pp. 52, 55 *et seq.*, 57.

[39] Si Wǫrawat, *Phongsawadan Phathalung*, pp. 72 *et seq.*

[40] Although it must be said that this rank was not always the title of the governor of Phathalung.

[41] *Phu chui yai.*

[42] Details in Si Wǫrawat, *op. cit.*, footnote 8, p. 72.

All higher officials had secretaries, with titles such as *Rǫng Palat*, *Rǫng Yokrabat*, *Khun Mŭn Rǫng Phu Chui* and *Khun Rǫng Phon.*

The king also nominated the *Luong Ča Burin Inthasena*, who handled the correspondence with the capital in accordance with the governor's instructions. He also administered the archives of the province. His assistant was the *Khun Ča* (*Khun Rǫng Ča*).

Appointments to all the remaining lower offices[43] were made by the governor as follows:

1. The "Quadruple Authority,"[44] consisting of:
   a. The "city administration"[45] under the *Luong Phetmontri Si Ratcha Wang Mŭang* who was responsible for the administration of the provincial city and the surrounding territory. In addition, he watched over the officials of the sub-districts, the Tambons. The *Luong Phetmontri* was also responsible for the investigation of capital crimes.
   b. The "palace guard administration"[46] under the *Luong Thepmonthien Na Wang*, who was in charge of the various ceremonies and was also responsible for accommodations for guests.
   c. The "treasury"[47] placed under the *Luong Inthamontri Si Ratcha Khlang*, which was responsible for the collection of the taxes, particularly such "natural" taxes as rice.
   d. The "agricultural authority"[48] under the *Luong Thepmontri Si Somphot Krom Na*, responsible for the irrigation and fertilizing of the ricefield, adequate provisions of rice for the population and the performance of the ploughing ceremony which indicated the beginning of the sowing.
2. The "office for penalties"[49] under the *Luong Intharaāya*, responsible for the punishment of relatively minor offenses.
3. The "office for civil affairs"[50] under the *Luong Phromsu-*

[43] *Kromakan phu nǫi* or *kromakan rǫng.*
[44] *Tamnaeng čatusadǫn.*
[45] *Wieng.*
[46] *Thepmonthien na wang.*
[47] *Khlang.*
[48] *Tamnaeng na.*
[49] *Tamnaeng aya.*
[50] *Tamnaeng phaeng.*

pha Phaen, responsible for disputes under civil law and the collection of claims.

4. The "office for statutory arrangements"[51] under the *Khun Saraphakọn*, which was a sort of lower court preliminary to offices (2) and (3). It received claims and accusations in cases of legal offenses and reported them to the governor, who, according to the nature of the case, instructed the appropriate court to take the matter in hand.
5. The "office for provisions and arms"[52] under the *Luong Chaiyasurin (phromsurin)*. The latter was responsible for the supervision of the government warehouses and also had to see to it that necessary supplies of arms and other equipment were available. He was also competent to receive gunpowder from the population. This was offered as a substitute for military service.
6. The "registry office"[53] under the *Luong Phichai Senasatsadi Klilang*. Here were kept the military roll and the list of those liable for poll tax, both now and in the future. The *Luong Intharasena Phu Chui*, *Luong Thepsenasatsadi Khwa*, *Luong Chaiya Khwa Satasadi Sai* and the *Luong Chaiyaseni Phu Chui* were assigned to the office in the capacity of assistants. Civil servants of inferior standings, *Khun Mŭn*, also kept lists of the receipts of other offices.
7. The "office for ceremonies"[54] under the *Luong Thepmonthien* had a general responsibility for the performance of ceremonies when these became due. For this purpose a large retinue, including twenty musicians, was at his disposal.
8. The "office for the departments of the governor's household":[55]

   a. The *Luong Klang Wang*[56] superintended the governor's housekeeping and the *Luong Thai Wang*[57] was in charge of his boats, vessels, horses and elephants.

[51] *Tamnaeng phra thammanun.*
[52] *Tamnaeng phatdusanphawut.*
[53] *Tamnaeng satsadi.*
[54] *Phanakngan phithi.*
[55] *Kromakan samrap pen phanakngan khọng čau mŭang.*
[56] "Officer for the head governor's palace."
[57] "Officer for the objects behind the governor's palace."

b. The *Phanakngan Wen Bon*,[58] together with four officials, was responsible for the accommodation and service of the guests of the governor and also had the task of keeping their weapons and articles of everyday use in good order.
c. The *Phanakngan Wen Lang*,[59] also under the authority of four officials, was responsible for the guard of the gates to the governor's palace, for the announcement of the time by means of a gong once every three hours, and also for the training of workers for such heavy tasks as sowing, changing the course of water or collecting wood.
d. The "scribe"[60] was the head of the department of writing and prepared all necessary written documents for the governor.
e. The *Khun Phiphitthaphakdi Čang Wang*[61] had all the personal servants of the governor under his direction.

9. The "office of special duties,"[62] with its numerous employees, always had to be available for exceptional occasions.
10. A province was divided into several districts, *Tambon's*, the heads of which, *Nai Tambon*, were appointed by the governor. Within his more restricted area of authority the *Nai Tambon* had administrative tasks similar to those of the governor, although the most important part of his work concerned the supervision and coordination of agriculture, particularly with regard to irrigation works. Every person able to work had to lay out and maintain from four to six meters of ditches and dikes in the paddy fields. In its method of work the village community had developed into a cooperative.[63]

Technically speaking, the officials received no salary; instead, everyone who was associated with a particular agency kept for himself a part of the income received by the agency. Moreover, royal rewards were distributed whenever there was a special reason.[64]

[58] Literal translation uncertain.
[59] Literal translation uncertain.
[60] *Luong supmatra.*
[61] Literal translation uncertain.
[62] *Kromakan phisek.*
[63] Si Wǫrawat, *op. cit.*, p. 78.
[64] Damrong, *Tamnan phasi akǫn*, p. 8.

There were special regulations for civil servants. By 1782, the year of the accession of Rama I to the throne, a decree was promulgated[65] forbidding all civil servants to participate in gambling. Anyone guilty of an infringement of this prohibition was liable to be beaten with a cudgel thrice thirty times and be deprived of all honors and positions. The gambling house proprietors, either Thai or Chinese, responsible for leading the officials astray could expect thirty cudgellings. In a further law of 1794 these regulations were set forth in detail and all forbidden games were precisely specified.[66] The thought behind this prohibition was that it is immoral to gain money by gambling; moreover, the money did not come from the owners of the gambling houses. The truth of the matter was that the players sold their wives, their children and, indeed, their whole property in order to indulge in their passion for gambling.[67] In law number 19 of the year 1795[68] there is a report of a case of this kind from Čanthaburi which was a subject of judicial treatment.

From the laws it is clear that the gambling houses were not generally closed—fiscal considerations alone would have made that impossible—but special regulations for civil servants were to be created. Other kinds of contests from which the state gained no material advantage and which were contrary to Buddhist commandments, for example, cockfighting, were generally forbidden.[69]

Beyond the hierarchy of civil servants stood the Buddhist clergy, *khana song*, under the *Phra Khru Ariya Sangwǫn* as head, *Čau Khana*.[70] The latter had at his disposal four deputies as well as four additional monks of higher rank for the ceremonies.

The entire province was under the supervision of the minister for South Thailand, the Kalahom, but at the same time other ministries in Bangkok were competent to give instructions regarding various matters. This overlapping of areas of authority naturally involved a certain degree of dissension, yet in view of the general situation prevailing at that time it may be said that the administration was, on the whole, well organized.

Royal decrees were transmitted through the registry office[71] to the

[65] *Pramuon kotmai ratchakan thi nüng*, vol. 3, *Phraratcha kamnot mai 2*.
[66] *Ibid.*, vol. 3, pp. 389 *et seq.*
[67] Damrong, *Tamnan loek bǫnbie*, p. 14.
[68] *Pramuon kotmai ratchakan thi nüng*, vol. 3, pp. 372 *et seq.*
[69] *Ibid.*, vol. 3, pp. 396 *et seq.*, *Kamnot mai 27*, among others.
[70] See also Vella, *Siam under Rama III 1824–1851*, pp. 33 *et seq.*
[71] *Krom phra suratsawadi.*

provinces and municipalities. There they were read to the people who were called together for this purpose by the sounding of a gong.[72] Copies of these decrees were kept in the *Hǫ Luong*,[73] the *Sala Luk Khun*[74] and in the *Sala Luong*.[75]

A fine document from the time of Rama I bearing on the ethics of the state and the duties of provincial administration is a circular letter of the Phraya Kalahom to the civil servants in the province of Nakhǫn Si Thammarat on the occasion of the nomination of Čau Phat as the new governor. This document,[76] dated the eleventh day of the waning moon in the eighth month 2327 (1784) has the following contents:[77]

Nakhǫn Si Thammarat has belonged to Thailand since the Ayuthaya epoch. After long wars the time has now come for a new governor to take over the administration of the province, and Čau Phat has been chosen for this purpose. He is to be greeted and received in the manner appropriate to his rank; and the people must be obedient to his will, for he will administer the province with justice. Restiveness will not be tolerated. [More detailed warnings about various illegalities follow, particularly with regard to robberies.] The governor has been sent in order to establish order. The population must not do anything harmful to the country.

Hereafter follow instructions[78] that the fortifications, gates and cannon were to be checked; moreover, arms, ammunition, various other objects and ships should be available in the necessary amounts and numbers. Ships should not be left exposed on the water when not in use, for sheds should be built for them. There is also a warning about Annamese pirates who were active there at that time. If the Annamese should manage to inflict injury on the city, either on its people or on objects in it, the governor and the responsible officials would be punished.

Generally speaking, the southern borderland was not yet pacified. For this reason, there should be new contingents of troops in training and one should always be prepared to fight. When hostilities arise one

[72] *Ti khǫng rǫng pau*, see Damrong, *Prapheni prakat*, p. 132.
[73] "Royal apartment."
[74] "Law court."
[75] "Assembly hall for ministers (and library)."
[76] *Santra.*
[77] *Tang čau phraya Nakhǫn Si Thammarat*, pp. 33 *et seq.*
[78] *Ibid.*, pp. 38 *et seq.*

should immediately attack if the troops are strong enough to do this; otherwise, that is to say, in a case where the "Indians"[79] have superior forces, one should request help from the surrounding provinces. At that time a state of war was still going on, and therefore everything and everyone should be kept in a state of preparedness. Those who distinguished themselves in battle were to be made commanders.

Between the governor and the officials there should be no discord which could prove harmful to the country. All occurrences were to be examined and investigated with fairness, and justice could be administered only in accordance with the laws. The officials should be careful not to show any partiality for reasons of personal favor, anger, fear or ignorance. On the contrary, their behavior should be exemplary and conform to the teachings of the Buddha.

Taxes and revenue administration

In principle the tax system of the first rulers of the Čakri dynasty was the same as that of the Ayuthaya and Thonburi epochs.[80] Taxes, customs duties and commercial profits were principal sources of revenue of the state. There were the following taxes: the alcohol tax,[81] the tax on gambling,[82] duty on goods brought to the market,[83] the so-called "water-tax"[84] which had to do with fishing and was calculated on the basis of fishing tackle, a tax which was levied on certain fruit trees[85] and other plants, and a garden or field tax[86] which was levied on land and which had to be paid with rice. However, all these taxes together did not amount to very much.[87]

The most important source of revenue was the profit from trade with China,[88] a trade which from Bangkok and other harbors was carried on with *samphans*.[89] Furthermore, every inhabitant of the kingdom between the ages of eighteen and seventy, with the exception of

[79] *Khaek*, apparently from Malay and the bordering Insulinde.
[80] Damrong, *Tamnan phasi akǫn*, p. 7.
[81] *Akǫn sura.*
[82] *Akǫn bǫnbie.*
[83] *Akǫn khanon talat.*
[84] *Kha nam* (*tam khruong mŭ*).
[85] *Akǫn somphatsǫn.*
[86] *Akǫn suon.*
[87] *P.P.R.I*, p. 346; *P.P.*, p. 464.
[88] See Skinner, *op. cit.*, pp. 25 *et seq.*, and Fairbank and Teng, *op. cit.*, p. 199.
[89] For these trading vessels a uniform flag was first prescribed during the time of Rama I; see Ankhong, *Thong chat*, p. 354; compare also Damrong, *Rŭang thong Thai*, p. 1.

the Buddhist monks, had to pay a poll tax,[90] which was now collected in a very different way. Under Rama I there was a general change from the system of discharging one's obligations to the state by work and services[91] to the payment of taxes in money. The amount of the taxes was also changed. Instead of the six months of service previously required the time of service was now fixed at three months; moreover, a monthly payment of six *bat* could now be substituted for it.[92] The duty to render service to the state was directly connected with the military service,[93] and in time of war the latter took the place of the former. For the rest there were no reforms in military organization during the time of Rama I.[94]

2. The New Codification of the Common Law From the Ayuthaya Epoch in 1805

The new codification of Thai laws inherited from the Ayuthaya epoch must be considered one of the most significant matters at the behest of Rama I in the course of the restoration of his country. From a decree of the king dated in the year 1794[95] it is known that at the time of the destruction of Ayuthaya nine-tenths of the legal manuscripts, that is to say, nine-tenths of the legal materials available at that time, were destroyed. Under these circumstances a stocktaking and a new codification naturally followed. However, the necessary work did not begin before 1804. The occasion was provided by a divorce case from Nakhọn Si Thammarat which was put before the king through the governor and the Čau Phraya Phra Khlang. The plaintiff was a certain Nai Bunsi, who urged that the divorce for which his wife, Amdaeng, applied and which had been granted by the law court could not be legally valid.[96] The judgment was based on the following facts. Ac-

[90] Quaritch-Wales, *Ancient Siamese Government and Administration*, pp. 199 *et seq.*; Vella, *Siam under Rama III 1824–1851*, pp. 19 *et seq.*; Damrong, *Tamnan phasi akọn*, pp. 7 *et seq.*; Si Wọrawat, *op. cit.*, p. 79.

[91] Which had been legally defined under Phra Narai (1657–1688).

[92] Damrong, *Tamnan phasi akọn*, p. 8.

[93] Damrong, *Tamnan ken thahan*, pp. 48 *et seq.*

[94] On all points reference may be obtained to the statements in Quaritch-Wales, *Ancient Siamese Government and Administration*, pp. 135 *et seq.*, which are largely based on Damrong's *Tamnan ken thahan.*

[95] *Phra ratcha kamnot mai 28*, in *Pramuon kotmai ratchakan thi nưng*, vol. 3, pp. 398 *et seq.*; see *ibid.*, p. 339, at the end.

[96] *Pramuon kotmai ratchakan thi nưng*, vol. 1, *Prakat phraratchaprarop*, p. 2; Dhani Nivat, "The Reconstruction of Rama I of the Chakry Dynasty," p. 27;

cording to the regulations in force during 1804[97] a married woman could demand a divorce at any time with the consequence that all the property which she had before her marriage was then to be returned to her. On the other hand, the husband could also demand a divorce in case of adultery on the part of his wife. In this case the plaintiff received her entire property. In the present case it was the wife of Nai Bunsi who demanded the divorce, although she had been guilty of adultery; and, moreover, this had been with one of the judges who had played a part in the granting of the divorce. Against this obvious perversion of justice Nai Bunsi urged that, although he was innocent, his wife could have a divorce involving the usual arrangements concerning property favorable to her.

The king shared the plaintiff's opinion that the sentence was not just. He therefore commanded that the available legal texts should be compared, *i.e.*, the three authentic editions which were kept in the law court, in the royal apartment and in the assembly hall for the ministers.[98] All three editions contained the same text, according to which the above-mentioned judgment had been pronounced. Rama I thereupon commanded that a committee should be appointed to examine the whole body of common law and codify it anew.

The committee consisted of the following eleven persons:[99] four royal secretaries,[100] of whom Khun Sunthǫn Wohan was chairman, three judges[101] and four jurists.[102] The meetings of the committee took place in the law court.

On the express instruction of the king, the laws were, above all, to be examined with regard to their agreement with the Pali canon, and in cases where they did not agree they were to be altered accordingly, in order to restore what was believed to be the original text.[103] Injustices in the law were to be attributed primarily to disloyal and dishonest officials who were more interested in material profits for themselves

Dhani Nivat, *Phra Phuttha Yǫt Fa songfŭnfu wathanathamm*, p. 35; Lingat, "Note sur la Révision des Lois Siamoises," *Journal of the Siam Society*, vol. 23, pp. 19 *et seq.*

[97] These can no longer be examined as earlier available texts were destroyed after the revision of 1804, see p. 37 below.

[98] Compare on this point footnotes 73–75 of this chapter.

[99] See *Pramuon kotmai ratchakan thi nŭng*, vol. 1, *Prakat phraratcha prawat*, p. 4.

[100] *Alaksana.*

[101] *Luk khun.*

[102] *Ratchabanthit.*

[103] *P.P.R.I*, p. 317; *P. P.*, p. 437.

than in the preservation of the law. These officials had falsified the laws for it was deemed impossible that the former kings of Thailand had made unjust rulings.[104]

The purpose, therefore, was not to introduce a new system of law or to subject the laws to a textual criticism, but to go back to the original laws by eliminating all the falsifications which had occurred since that time. The extent to which this objective was achieved as well as the methods of work which were used[105] are matters which cannot be definitely ascertained on the basis of the material available today. The legal texts valid before 1804 which served as a foundation for the committee on revision have not been preserved. They may even have been deliberately destroyed in order to emphasize that from that time on only the new texts were to be considered valid.[106] Moreover, when one considers the tremendous loss of handwritten legal texts resulting from the destruction of Ayuthaya it is virtually certain that it will never be possible for scholars to restore the original texts of the Ayuthaya epoch. It is possible that a part of the lost nine-tenths of the old Ayuthaya laws, which were no longer available for revision, were put into the new codex of laws. The remains of the old Ayuthaya laws as given in the book of laws of 1805 are all that we have today for information about the law as it might have been in Thailand at an earlier period.[107] There can be no reasonable doubt concerning the authenticity of the contents of these texts, to be sure, and as they are the only documents of this kind which have come down to us, they are indeed of inestimable value for the study of law and sociology during the Ayuthaya epoch.

The work of the committee lasted only eleven months. Because of this relatively short period of time, one may doubt whether the entire codex in the form in which we have it today was newly classified. One is justified to suppose that the old division was taken over, beginning

[104] *Pramuon kotmai ratchakan thi nüng*, vol. 1, *Prakat phraratcha prawat*, pp. 3, 4; see also Lingat, "Note sur la Révision des Lois Siamoises en 1805," p. 21.

[105] Whether the statements of Damrong are valid with regard to the revision of 1804 (in *Tamnan kotmai müang Thai*, p. 5 f.) seems doubtful.

[106] See Dhani Nivat, "The Reconstruction of Rama I of the Chakry Dynasty," p. 28.

[107] On the legal history of the Ayuthaya epoch see in particular Damrong, *Tamnan kotmai müang Thai*, pp. 16 *et seq.;* Nitisatphaisan, *Prawatsat kotmai Thai*, pp. 139 *et seq.; Masao, "Researches into Indigenous Law of Siam as a Study of Comparative Jurisprudence,"* pp. 14 *et seq.;* Lingat, "Evolution of the Conception of Law in Burma and Siam," pp. 9 *et seq*. Research in this field is still at the stage of conjectures.

with the *Phra Thammasat*.[108] Every proposed change had to be put before the king, who himself decided what would be right for the country.[109]

After the revision of the texts was completed copies were put for safekeeping in the law court, in the royal apartment and in the assembly hall for ministers; and these copies were sealed three times.[110] Each of them was accepted as an authentic text.[111]

In addition to this partial restoration of the law which had been handed down, Rama I showed himself to be a legislator in his own right. No less than forty-five laws and decrees[112] have come down to us.[113] In 1782, the year of the king's succession to the throne, three laws had already been made[114] which concerned the following:

1. The command that civil servants of all ranks from the highest to the lowest should take the necessary precautions for the security of the king on the occasion of his departure.
2. Greater severity in the disciplinary cudgelling of civil servants participating in gambling activities.
3. Amendments to the punitive regulations for thieves.

By far the greatest part of the legislation of the following years also had to do with penal regulations and prohibitions for the civil servants.

3. The Revision of the Buddhist Canon and the Council in Bangkok, 1788

Upon taking over the government Rama I immediately applied himself to the task of making important changes in rank among the

[108] More detailed information on the *Phra Thammasat* is to be found in Dhani Nivat, *Phra Phuttha Yǫt Fa songfŭnfu wathanathamm*, pp. 37 *et seq.;* Dhani Nivat, "The Old Siamese Conception of the Monarchy," pp. 91 *et seq.;* Nitisatphaisan, *op. cit.*, pp. 82 *et seq.*

[109] *P.P.R.I*, p. 318; *P.P.*, p. 437.

[110] With the seal of the lion, *ratchasiha*, the proboscis lion, *khochasiha*, and the diamond lotus, *bua kaeo*. After this sealing the law codex is designated as *Chabap luong tra sam duong*, "Royal Codes of the Three Seals."

[111] See the statements in Lingat, *Kham nam*, pp. 2–5.

[112] *Kamnot*, which seems to mean "decree with the force of law"; in *Pramuon kotmai ratchakan thi nŭng*, vol. 3, pp. 311 *et seq.*, described as *Phraratcha kamnot mai*, "New Royal Decrees."

[113] The question whether everything has come down to us cannot be answered, compare Nitisatphaisan, *op. cit.*, pp. 207 *et seq.*

[114] Dhani Nivat, *Phraphuttha Yǫt Fa songfŭnfu wathanathamm*, p. 47, states that in 2325 (1782) nine laws were enacted by Rama I, but the collection of laws itself does not make it possible to reach this conclusion.

Buddhist hierarchy of the country. Under Taksin a large number of unworthy persons had been promoted to high positions in the clergy. At the command of Rama I such persons were now expelled from the community of Buddhist monks,[115] or at least degraded to inferior positions.[116] The king saw to it that all complaints about moral offenses or punishable actions on the part of the monks were properly investigated.[117] On the other hand, monks who, under Taksin, had been deprived of their positions for no good reason were now reinstated.

The position of a Thai king in relation to the Buddhist hierarchy of his country should not be misinterpreted as that of a head priest. His mission was rather to promote and protect Buddhism,[118] that is to say, he had to guard against decay from within and simultaneously ward off attacks from outside. During the first two years after his accession to the throne Rama I issued seven decrees concerning the Buddhist monks in Thailand.[119] Their purpose was to raise the moral level of this class and to restore its prestige and authority. In addition, one more law was passed in each of the following years, 1789, 1794 and 1801.[120] The Last law, the tenth, expelled 128 monks from the Buddhist clergy and condemned them to hard labor for "they had been guilty of all kinds of ignoble behavior, namely drinking, wandering about at night, rubbing shoulders with women, using improper language, buying silly things from Chinese junks."[121]

Decrees were expressly issued for the civil servants and for the remaining population in order to keep them to a correct Buddhist way of life.[122] In one of the decrees the king concerned himself with various widespread ideas of a superstitious nature[123] with particular reference to the civil servants. Offerings such as flowers, fruit and candles could still be made as in the past, but not in excessive amounts and not as an

[115] *P.P.*, p. 200.

[116] *Ibid.*, p. 210.

[117] See for example *ibid.*, p. 210.

[118] Dhani Nivat, "The Reconstruction of Rama I of the Chakry Dynasty," pp. 26 *et seq.*; Dhani Nivat, "The Old Siamese Conception of the Monarchy," pp. 91 *et seq.* Compare also Article 4 of Constitution of Siam 2475 and the corresponding articles in the subsequent constitutions, for example, collected and translated in Wenk, *Die Verfassungen Thailands*, pp. 21, 28, 38, 49, 69.

[119] *Kot phra song, Pramuon kotmai ratchakan thi nŭng*, vol. 3, pp. 1–35.

[120] *Ibid.*, vol. 3, pp. 36–49, 49–51, 51–56; compare Dhani Nivat, *Phraphuttha Yǫt Fa songfŭnfu wathanathamm*, pp. 16 *et seq.*

[121] *Pramuon kotmai ratchakan thi nŭng*, vol. 3, pp. 52 *et seq.*

[122] *Phraratcha kamnot mai 2* and *13*, in *ibid.*, vol. 3, pp. 315 *et seq.*, pp. 353 *et seq.*; see also Dhani Nivat, *Phra Phuttha Yǫt Fa songfŭnfu wathanathamm*, pp. 24 *et seq.*

[123] *Phraratcha kamnot mai 35*, in *Pramuon kotmai ratchakan thi nŭng*, vol. 3, pp. 417–422.

expression of Buddhist belief. The killing of animals was forbidden in any case.[124]

Mention has already been made above of the construction of Buddhist temples in Bangkok. In other places also the king had new temples built or older ones restored, and, in particular, the temple Phra Phuthabat, the "Temple of Buddha's Footprint" at Saraburi, one of the most famous shrines of Thailand. Taksin had begun reconstruction at Saraburi but had not been able to complete it.[125] In 1787, after the second Burmese invasion, Rama I charged the Maha Uparat with the rebuilding of the Monthop in the same style in which it had been constructed under Phra Bǫrǫmakot.

One of the chief preoccupations of Rama I during his reign was the purification and editing of the Buddhist Canon in order to produce a partly new version. With this in mind he called together a council in Bangkok in 1788.[126] Previously the king had already had manuscripts of the Tripitaka collected in the Lao and Mǫn versions[127] and had them rewritten in Khǫm.[128] These Khǫm versions were studied by the priesthood in the preparation of the council. After a certain Čamŭn Wayawǫranat had pointed out that many volumes differed from each other and that it was not known which text was the correct one, the king gave the command to call together a council at Bangkok in order to restore the original text of the canon.[129]

With the Maha Uparat as chairman, the members of the council assembled in the throne hall. Most members of the royal family were present, as well as the Buddhist patriarch of Thailand, monks and a hundred Buddhist scholars. The king had food and gifts allotted to each person present and then asked the assembled clergy whether the Tripiṭaka at hand was as it should be or whether it differed from the right text. Therefore the patriarch answered that the texts of this canon differed from one another and needed to be revised.[130]

[124] *Ibid.*, p. 419.

[125] *P.P.R.I*, p. 157; see also *Khun Khlǫn, Khamhaikan*, and Damrong, *Phrabat*, pp. 72 *et seq.;* details on the building in Buribhand, *The Buddha's Footprint*, pp. 16 *et seq.*

[126] Narinthewi, *op. cit.*, p. 216; see also Coedès, *The Vajirañâna National Library*, pp. 21 *et seq.*

[127] *P.P.R.I*, p. 183.

[128] Thai version of "Khmer."

[129] In *P.P.R.I*, p. 183; and in *P.P.*, p. 303, the *Phra Pali* and the *Atthagathadika* (a commentary to the *Phra Pali*) are mentioned; *Phra Pali* means all Buddhist scriptures which are written in the common language of Hînayâna Buddhism, *i.e.*, Pali.

[130] *P.P.R.I*, pp. 184 *et seq.* Thiphakarawong also deals with the history of Buddhism and its diffusion in Thailand; *item P.P.*, pp. 305 *et seq.*

On the basis of this statement Rama I commanded that the texts should be revised. Two hundred and eighteen monks and thirty-two Buddhist scholars[131] were appointed for this task. The king, the Maha Uparat and the entire court were present at the opening ceremony of the council, which began with a solemn procession. Under the direction of the patriarch the council was then divided into four working committees. The patriarch himself took over the chairmanship of the committee on revision of the *Phra Sutrapiṭaka;*[132] Phra Wanarat became chairman of the committee on revision of the *Phra Vinayapiṭaka;*[133] Phra Phimonlathamm[134] took over the committee for the purification of the *Phra Satawiset,*[135] and Phra Thammatrailok[136] for the purification of the *Paramatthapiṭaka.*[137]

The committees met in various rooms of the Wat Mahathat, the seat of the patriarch.[138] According to the records all the available texts were examined and all deviations were rectified.[139] Doubtful matters were put before a commission having special authority which then reached a decision. After about five months the work of the committees came to an end. The revised texts[140] were written on palmleaf manuscripts; and, after they were gilded on the outside, the manuscripts were kept in a building with a fortified wall expressly constructed for this purpose, *Phra Monthop.*[141]

All who took part in the council received clothing and other gifts from the king, who also defrayed all living expenses of the council during the five months of its duration.[142]

[131] *Ratchabanthit ačan.*

[132] Pali: *Sutta-Piṭaka.*

[133] Pali: *Vinaya-Piṭaka.*

[134] *P.P.R.I*, p. 193; *P.P.*, p. 313, gives here another name: *Phra Aphithamm.*

[135] *Phra satthawiset,* "grammatical treatise." I do not know to which part of the Buddhist scriptures this refers.

[136] According to *P.P.*, p. 312: Phra Phuthačau.

[137] *Phra paramatthapiṭaka: paramat,* "highest perfection," by which the *Abhidhamma-piṭaka* is meant.

[138] Compare Damrong, *Prawat athibọdi song nai Wat Mahathat*, pp. 1 *et seq.*

[139] *P.P.R.I*, p. 194.

[140] To what extent and on the basis of what criteria a revision of the text was undertaken are open questions, concerning which—in my opinion—there has not yet been any research on the part of Buddhist scholars. But it is doubtful whether sufficient documents are still available to make it possible to properly investigate the work of the Council of 1788. (The edition of the *Tripiṭaka* generally accepted in Thailand today has forty-five volumes, each of about 500 pages.)

[141] Narinthewi, *op. cit.*, p. 221; for further details of a purely formal nature concerning the *Tripiṭaka* manuscripts, see Čulalongkọn, *Phraratchawitčan*, pp. 217 *et seq.*; *P.P.R.I*, pp. 196 *et seq.*

[142] According to Dhani Nivat, *Phra Phutha Yọt Fa songfŭnfu wathanathamm*, p. 11, and Chakrabongse, *op. cit.*, p. 86, from the personal funds of the king. But

And during the later years of his reign, Rama I, as a devout believer in Buddhist doctrine, was always careful to promote the purity of Buddhism and of the monkhood.

In 1797 a new patriarch was appointed,[143] and prior to 1809 numerous temples were constructed in the new capital city. The decoration of these temples with famous statues of the Buddha was one of the principal preoccupations of the king.[144]

such statements are true only in a limited sense as during the time of Rama I in practice, indeed even in theory, no distinction was made between government resources and the king's personal possessions.

[143] *P.P.R.I*, p. 241.

[144] *Ibid.*, pp. 246 *et seq.*; *P.P.*, pp. 366 *et seq.*, 458.

Chapter IV

THE RESTORATION OF THE EXTERNAL SPHERES OF INFLUENCE

1. The Burmese Wars. The Defense of the Western and Northern Boundaries, 1785–1802.

The campaign of 1785. The battle with the Burmese main army and the battle of Lat Ya

About three years after the beginning of the reign of Rama I, it became very clear that the Burmese were planning a new attack on Thailand on a large scale. The Mǫn, who lived in the borderland near Burma and who had been appointed as spies,[1] brought the first news of this to Bangkok. Then similar reports came from the Kančanaburi and from the other provincial governors of northern and southern Thailand, from Chumphǫn, Thalang, Ratburi, Tak, Kamphaengphet, Phitsanulok, Sukhothai and Sawannkhalok. It was reported that the Burmese had assembled at Martaban and that they were already under way.[2]

The fact that the Burmese had not taken advantage of the opportunity to attack provided by the confusion around the throne in Bangkok in 1782 is probably to be explained by the serious internal political problems with which Burma was faced at that time.[3]

According to both Thai and Burmese records, offers to negotiate preceded the Burmese war preparations.[4] From a letter dated 1793,[5]

[1] Damrong, *Thai rop Phama*, vol. 2, p. 173.

[2] *P.P.*, p. 239; *P.P.R.I*, p. 111.

[3] *Phongsawadan Mǫn Phama*, p. 380; *P.P.*, p. 215; Damrong, *Thai rop Phama*, vol. 2, p. 170; *P.P.R.I*, p. 107; Harvey, *History of Burma From the Earliest Times to 10th March 1824*, pp. 264 *et seq.;* Sangermano, *A Description of the Burmese Empire*, pp. 50 *et seq.;* Phraison Salarak, "Intercourse between Burma and Siam, as recorded in Hmannam Yazawindawgyi," pp. 1 *et seq.*

[4] *Čerača khuam mŭang Thai Phama*, p. 3; Sonakun, *Prawatsat Thai samai krung ratanakosin yuk raek*, p. 40; *P.P.R.I*, p. 236; *P.P.*, p. 357; Phraison Salarak, *op. cit.*, pp. 12 *et seq.*

[5] Referred to in *Čerača khuam mŭang Thai Phama*, p. 3.

addressed by the governor of Kančanaburi to the Burmese, one may assume that in the year of the Great Dragon *Č.S.* 1146 (1784) the latter had negotiated with the Thai in the Tambon Angngiu with a view to establishing friendly relations between the two states. However, according to the Burmese *Hmannan Yazawindawgyi*, the initiative to negotiate came from the Thai.

In view of the internal political difficulties of the Burmese such an initiative on their part is quite possible, yet we have no evidence which would enable us to determine to what extent this attempt may have been seriously intended and authorized by the Burmese government. And, moreover, the Thai government was filled with a deep mistrust of its neighbors, so that matters probably did not reach the point of serious negotiations.[6]

In 1784[7] Bodawpaya,[8] the Burmese king, began to prepare the drawing up of his armies, which in 1785 were to invade Thailand with superior forces.[9] Accounts of the strength of the Burmese armies vary from 103,000 to 144,000.[10] Statements about the grouping and drawing up of the armies are also divergent, yet the records essentially agree with regard to the following details.

1. The first army under the command of Kaengwunmaengyi[11] was drawn up at Mergui with a total of

[6] In *ibid.*, note 5, pp. 4 *et seq.*, the negotiations are made out to be simply a ruse which, among other things, provided the opportunity for spying on the border by the Burmese envoys.

[7] *Khamhaikan chau angwa*, p. 19; according to *Khamhaikan Mahakho*, p. 27, it was in 1785 (2328).

[8] The Thai form of the Burmese king's name is Padung.

[9] See Phayre, *History of Burma*, pp. 215 *et seq.;* Phraison Salarak, *op. cit.*, p. 7.

[10] *P.P.R.I*, p. 111, refers to 103,000 men; *item* Čulalongkǫn *Phraratchawitčan*, p. 213, although the account given here, particularly with regard to the main forces under Bodawpaya, is by no means remarkable for clarity; *P.P.*, pp. 235 *et seq.*, refers to 130,000 men; Damrong, *Thai rop Phama*, vol. 2, p. 170, to 144,000; Symes, *An Account of an Embassy to the Kingdom of Ava . . . in the year 1795*, p. 264, working on a basis of much smaller numbers, reckons that the army of Bodawpaya had around 30,000 men, but it is not clear whether this figure includes the whole Burmese army or refers only to the main army; Phraison Salarak, *op. cit.*, pp. 1 *et seq.*, gives 104,000 men.

[11] *Phongsawadan Mǫn Phama*, p. 380; *P.P.*, p. 235; *P.P.R.I*, p. 107. Damrong, *Thai rop Phama*, vol. 2, p. 170, at first mentions Maengyi Maengkhǫngkayo as the general but then quotes the Burmese Phongsawadan, according to which the latter was put to death at the command of Bodawpaya, as he did not duly carry out the supply provisions of the main force which had been entrusted to him and in this way delayed its departure. Afterwards Kaengwunmaengyi was appointed commander of the first army. See also Phraison Salarak, *op. cit.*, pp. 7, 8, 13, in whose

10,000 men,[12] including both land and sea troops in addition to fifteen men-of-war.[13] The land troops with a vanguard of 2,500 men under Nemayokhungnarat[14] and with a main force of 4,500 under Kaengwunmaengyi were expected to advance from Mergui to Chumphǫn and Chaiya and from there to Songkhla. The remaining 3,000 naval troops were to attack the west coast of Thailand[15] from Takuapa to Thalang.[16]

2. The second army under Anǫkfaekkhitwun[17] was drawn up at Thavoi[18] with 10,000 land troops and was to push forward over Bǫngti (west of Kančanaburi) to Ratburi, Phetburi and on to Chumphǫn in order to meet the first army.[19] Part of these troops, 3,000 men, were placed under the command of the governor of Thavoi, Wun.[20] Another 3,000 were under the command of Čiksinbo and the remaining 4,000 directly under the order of Anǫkfaekkhitwunyi.
3. The third army, which may really be considered the main force, was under the command of Bodawpaya. Toward the end of 1784 he set out from Martaban with the intention of pushing forward directly to Bangkok over the shortest and

---

translation of the *Hmannan Yazawindawgyi* Maengyi Maengkhongkaya is called Mingyi Mingaung Kyaw and Kaengwunmaengyi is called Wungyi Maha Thiri Thihathu.

[12] The references given in footnote 11 agree on this as does also Čulalongkǫn, *Phraratchawitčan,* p. 212; Symes, *op. cit.*, p. 261, says 8,000, but compare to the end of footnote 13.

[13] Damrong, *Thai rop Phama,* vol. 2, p. 170; *P.P.R.I,* p. 107; see also *P.P.*, p. 235; according to Harvey, *op. cit.*, p. 271, eleven warships participated in this action, led by Portuguese halfcastes; Symes, *op. cit.*, p. 260, agrees, but it is questionable whether his statements can be verified with regard to chronology. Symes, p. 264, reckons the southern fleet which was drawn up together with the main force of Bodawpaya at sixteen ships.

[14] In Damrong, *Thai rop Phama,* vol. 2, p. 187, called Nemayokhanǫngra; in *P.P.*, p. 235, Natmilaeng, Baetongča, Palingbo, Natčakkibo and Tǫngphayungbo are also mentioned as commanders.

[15] In order to stop alleged shipments of weapons from India, according to Phayre, *op. cit.*, p. 215, who considers this undertaking senseless.

[16] The previous capital of Phuket.

[17] Another form in *P.P.*, p. 235: Anǫkphaekdikwun; and in *Phongsawadan Mǫn Phama,* p. 380: Anǫkfaektikuwun; Phraison Salarak, *op. cit.*, p. 13: Nemyo Nawrata Kyawdin.

[18] According to *P.P.*, p. 236; also in Martaban, apparently in order to cross the mountains at the border from this point.

[19] *P.P.R.I,* p. 108; Damrong, *Thai rop Phama,* vol. 2, p. 171.

[20] *P.P.*, p. 235.

traditional pathway, the Pass of the Three Pagodas, and then over Kančanaburi. Accounts of the strength of this army differ considerably.[21] The advance guard under Mienwun may have had around 10,000 men.[22] Moreover, three reserve armies went before the main contingent. One was under Mienmewun with 5,000 men;[23] another under Takhaengkama[24] (the third son of Bodawpaya) with around 10,000 men;[25] and a third under the second son of Bodawpaya, Takhaengčakku,[26] also with about 10,000 men.[27] Bodawpaya followed with the main body of the army. Here again reports on its size vary from 10,000 to 50,000 men.[28] And this main force was divided into an advance guard, a left wing, a right wing and a rear guard.

4. The fourth army under Čokhongnaratha,[29] starting from Martaban, intended to push forward toward central Thailand in the direction of Tak. Its objective was to take the cities at the Mae Phing and then by way of Kamphaeng-

[21] Damrong, *Thai rop Phama*, vol. 2, p. 171: 89,000 men, *item P.P.R.I*, pp. 108 *et seq.; P.P.*, p. 236: 50,000 men, yet if one adds up all the troop contingents mentioned here the resulting sum is 55,000. Unclear statements are also found in Čulalongkǫn, *Phraratchawitčan*, p. 212, who, to be sure, fixes the main force at 45,000 men but whose calculations are questionable—compare footnote 10 of this chapter. See also *Phongsawadan Mǫn Phama*, 380, and Chakrabongse, *Lords of Life*, p. 98, whose figures are probably too low; Phraison Salarak, *op. cit.:* 50,000 men.

[22] *Khamhaikan chau angwa*, p. 21. According to Damrong, *Thai rop Phama*, vol. 2, p. 171, and *P.P.R.I*, p. 108: 11,000 men; in *P.P.R.I*, the commander is given as Miengwunmaengyi Mahathimkhong; in *Phongsawadan Mǫn Phama*, p. 380, by Miowun the herewith mentioned Mienwun is probably meant and by Mienwun the commander of the first reserve army Mienmewun.

[23] Damrong, *Thai rop Phama*, vol. 2, p. 171, remarks here that in the Burmese chronicle this army is not noted down, though this chronicle otherwise agrees with all Thai records.

[24] According to *Khamhaikan chau angwa*, p. 21: Kamasakhaeng.

[25] Damrong, *Thai rop Phama*, vol. 2, p. 171, and *P.P.R.I*, p. 109: 12,000 men; in *P.P.R.I*, there is the further statement that Takhaengkama was the second son of Bodawpaya.

[26] According to *Khamhaikan chau angwa*, p. 21: Čakkusakhaeng.

[27] *P.P.R.I*, p. 109, and Damrong, *Thai rop Phama*, vol. 2, p. 171: 11,000 men; according to *P.P.R.I*, Takhaengčakku was the third son of Bodawpaya, but *Phongsawadan Mǫn Phama*, p. 380, and *P.P.*, p. 236, do not agree on this point.

[28] Damrong, *Thai rop Phama*, p. 172: 50,000 men; Čulalongkǫn, *Phraratchawitčan*, p. 212: 10,000 men; *P.P.R.I*, p. 109, and *P.P.*, p. 236: 20,000 men; *Khamhaikan chau angwa*, p. 21: 25,000 men. Phayre, *op. cit.*, p. 210, also states "at least" 50,000 men, as does also Phraison Salarak, *op. cit.*, p. 8.

[29] *Phongsawadan Mǫn Phama*, p. 380: Čomongnǫratha; *P.P.*, p. 260, referred to as Chuitongweračongthaeng.

phet come together with the main army before Bangkok.[30] All reports agree that the strength of this army was 5,000 men.[31]

5. The fifth army under the command of the prince of Tǫng U, Sadomahasiriutčana,[32] advanced toward North Thailand. The point of departure of this army was probably Chiengsaen, which appears to have been the principal base of the Burmese at that time in the territory of the Lao States. Beginning from this point, the main part of the army, around 15,000 men, under Sadomahasiriutčana himself was to take Lampang; while at the same time another detachment with 5,000 men was to march down the Mae Nam Yom and conquer Sawannkhalok, Phitsanulok and Sukhothai. The remaining troops, chiefly Lao auxiliary forces under the governor of Chiengsaen, Aparakamani, were to advance in the direction of Čaehom. The ultimate objective of the northern army was to unite with the main force of Bodawpaya before Bangkok.[33] The total number of all troops under the command of Sadomahasiriutčana is variously given as between 23,000[34] and 50,000[35] men.

The strategy of Bodawpaya was fundamentally different from that of his predecessors. In the past it had been the custom of the Burmese to invade Thailand by only one or, at the most, two separate routes[36] in order to reach the plain of the Mae Nam Čau Phraya as rapidly as possible with a powerful and superior main force and to give the Thai no opportunity to prepare for the defense of certain mountain passes. Bodawpaya, on the contrary, divided his army into five parts, each part taking a different route, thereby depriving himself in advance of the advantages of being able to carry out a decisive military operation by

[30] Damrong, *Thai rop Phama*, vol. 2, p. 172.

[31] In the references already quoted.

[32] *P.P.*, p. 227: Sadomahasiriučana. Different form also in Damrong, *Thai rop Phama*, vol. 2, p. 171, and in *P.P.R.I*, p. 110. Phraison Salarak, *op. cit.*, p. 13: Wungyi Thado Thiri Maha Uzana.

[33] *Phongsawadan Mǫn Phama*, p. 380; *P.P.R.I*, p. 110; *P.P.*, p. 237; Damrong, *Thai rop Phama*, vol. 2, p. 171.

[34] *P.P.*, p. 237 *et seq.;* Čulalongkǫn, *Phraratchawitčan*, p. 212.

[35] Damrong, *Thai rop Phama*, vol. 2, p. 171, and *P.P.R.I*, p. 110: 30,000 men; *Khambaikan chau angwa*, p. 22: 50,000 men.

[36] On this point see the accounts of previous Burmese wars in Damrong, *Thai rop Phama*, vol. 1.

means of a single army greatly superior to the enemy.[37] This dispersion made it necessary to establish different supply centers on the widely separated routes of the various armies, an almost insoluble problem as the further course of the campaign was to prove. In the event of a rapid advance into the plain of the Mae Nam it would have been possible to provide for the needs of the Burmese army very largely from Thai supplies.

Upon receiving the news of the imminent invasion of the Burmese, Rama I called together an assembly of the leading civil and military officials.[38] Although we have no detailed information about the discussions which took place during this assembly we can probably form a fairly correct idea about them on the basis of the strategy decided upon. Rama I did not make the same mistake as his Burmese enemy, that is to say, he did not disperse his already weaker troops in the same manner as Bodawpaya. The decision was made to attack the enemy first with all possible strength at the place which seemed most important. This meant, above all, to prevent the main force led by Bodawpaya from crossing the mountains at the border and to hinder it from breaking through into the Mae Nam plain.[39]

This plan, essentially different from previous Thai strategy, was an innovation on the part of Rama I and his advisers. In the numerous past wars with Burma it had been the practice of the Thai, whenever they were inferior in numbers, to let the Burmese march in and not to join battle until they had arrived near Ayuthaya.[40] Only when the Thai had considered themselves strong enough had they attacked the enemy at a predetermined point, frequently in the vicinity of Suphanburi or, when the Burmese came from the north, at Angthong.[41]

The Thai armies were grouped as follows:

1. The first army was placed under the command of the future Krom Phraratcha Wang Lang,[42] to whom Krom Luong Narinthanaret, Čau Phraya Mahasena and the

[37] Sangermano, *op. cit.*, pp. 58 *et seq.*; Hall, *A History of South-East Asia*, pp. 503 *et seq.*

[38] *P.P.R.I*, p. 111; *P.P.*, p. 239.

[39] Damrong, *Thai rop Phama*, vol. 2, p. 174.

[40] As, for example, in the case of the invasions of Burengnong, see Damrong, *Phraprawat Somdet Phra Naresuon Maharat*, pp. 8 *et seq.*

[41] See Damrong, *Thai rop Phama*, vol. 2, p. 177.

[42] About that time, 1785, he, a nephew of Rama I, was still Čau Fa Krom Luong Anurakthewet. After this campaign he was raised to the rank of Phraratcha Wang Lang; see *P.P.R.I*, p. 133; Sommot Amǫraphan, *Chaloem phrayot čau nai*, p. 32.

Phraya Phra Khlang,[43] among others, had been assigned as officers. With approximately 15,000 men[44] this army was to be stationed at Nakhǫn Sawann in order to ward off the Burmese pressing down from the North, more precisely, in order to prevent them from pushing forward to Bangkok. At the same time the first army was to keep watch on the enemy marching over Kančanaburi and, if necessary, to fight against it also.[45]

2. The second army, in reality the main force, was under the command of the Maha Uparat and was drawn up with 30,000 men at Kančanaburi[46] in order to fight against the Burmese main force approaching by way of the Three Pagoda Pass.
3. The third army under the command of Čau Phraya Thammathibǫdi[47] and Čau Phraya Yomarat was drawn up with 5,000 men at Ratburi in order to keep the supply route for the main army open and in order to ward off the Burmese in case they should approach from the south or from Thavoi.
4. The fourth army of 20,000 men under the command of the king remained in Bangkok in reserve. It was to come to the aid of whichever army most needed help at any particular time.[48]

To sum up, approximately 70,000[49] Thai troops[50] were standing against the Burmese army.

The Maha Uparat set out in the first lunar month of 1784.[51] The

[43] *P.P.*, p. 240; *P.P.R.I*, p. 112; *Phongsawadan Mǫn Phama*, p. 381; Čulalongkǫn, *Phraratchawitčan*, p. 213.

[44] *P.P.R.I*, p. 114; *P.P.*, p. 242; and Damrong, *Thai rop Phama*, vol. 2, p. 174, agree on this point.

[45] Damrong, *Thai rop Phama*, vol. 2, p. 174; Phraison Salarak, *op. cit.*, p. 15, refers to a force of about 20,000 or 30,000 men "which was sent to Kanpuri."

[46] *P.P.R.I*, p. 113; *P.P.*, p. 240; *Phongsawadan Mǫn Phama*, p. 381.

[47] According to *P.P.R.I*, p. 114: Thammathikǫn.

[48] Damrong, *Thai rop Phama*, vol. 2, p. 175.

[49] According to Chakrabongse, *op. cit.*, p. 98: 50,000 men, but sources are not given.

[50] For general information on the organization of the Thai army see Damrong, *Tamnan ken thahan*, pp. 48, 50 *et seq.;* on equipment and arms see the discussions in *Phichai, Songkhram Thai*, pp. 1 *et seq.;* for similar information about the Burmese army see Symes, *op. cit.*, vol. 2, pp. 358 *et seq.*

[51] *P.P.R.I*, p. 112; Sonakun, *op. cit.*, pp. 21 *et seq.;* Chakrabongse, *op. cit.*, p. 98; Damrong, *Thai rop Phama*, vol. 2, p. 176.

necessary equipment for his army was watched over by the Phraya Kalahom, who, together with the Phraya Saenyakǫn, led the advance guard of this army.[52] Čau Fa Krom Luong Čakačetsada acted as "judge for martial affairs,"[53] Čau Phraya Ratanaphiphit as quartermaster,[54] and Phraya Monthienban led the rear guard. Most of the troops were transported by sea to Kančanaburi. They then built a fortified camp with ramparts and trenches in the plain of Lat Ya situated in the north and sloping off to the northwest. The flanks of the army were so far from one another that it was possible to contain the advancing Burmese troops in the difficult and narrow terrain.[55] If the Thai could hold on to their position at Lat Ya, then the remaining part of the way to Bangkok would be barred to the main force of the Burmese. The Burmese would then be obliged to halt at the jungle-covered mountain slopes arising from the plain. This would necessarily damage their marching order and their situation with regard to provisions and would, at the same time, reduce to a minimum their freedom of movement and ability to deploy their troops. It would then be up to the Thai to determine the outcome of the battle.

For purposes of observation the Phraya Maha Yotha was dispatched with 3,000 Mǫn troops[56] to a pass situated farther to the north at Kančanaburi on the Mae Nam Khwae Yai.

Meanwhile the Burmese vanguard under Mienwun advanced over the Pass of the Three Pagodas[57] over Saiyok, and into the valley of the Mae Nam Khwae Yai in the direction of Kram Chang. The Burmese, greatly superior in numbers, overran the Mǫn troops stationed there under Maha Yotha[58] and continued their march to Lat Ya, where the army of the Maha Uparat was waiting for them. The Burmese entrenched themselves against the Thai troops in a number of fortified encampments and awaited the arrival of the second vanguard contingent under Mienmewun. After its arrival they prepared for battle.

[52] *P.P.*, p. 241.

[53] *Yokrabat.*

[54] *Thi samuhanayok pen kiekkai*, *P.P.R.I*, p. 113.

[55] Damrong, *Thai rop Phama*, vol. 2, p. 176; *P.P.*, p. 241; *Phongsawadan Mǫn Phama*, p. 381; *P.P.R.I*, p. 113.

[56] Generally speaking, it appears that in this campaign the Mǫn were used by both the Thai and the Burmese as advance troops, perhaps to be explained by the fact that they were mistrusted by both sides as a frontier people.

[57] On the origin of the designation Three Pagoda Pass, see Damrong, *Phra čedi sam ǫng;* concerning the advancing of the Burmese main army see Phraison Salarak's translation of the *Hmannan Yazawindawgyi*, pp. 8 *et seq.*

[58] *P.P.R.I*, p. 114; *P.P.*, p. 242; Damrong, *Thai rop Phama*, vol. 2, p. 176. See also Phraison Salarak, *op. cit.*, p. 15.

Meanwhile, the remaining parts of the Burmese main force advanced. They were all obliged to encamp in the desolate mountain lands. The army under Takhaengkama at Tha Din Daeng, the army under Takhaengčakku at Sam Sop and the head army under Bodawpaya in the vicinity of the Pass of the Three Pagodas were all in a difficult predicament.[59] The direct consequence of this situation was that the whole Burmese army had to be supplied with provisions from Burma transported over mountain lands of difficult access.

As soon as the Maha Uparat was properly informed about the situation in which the Burmese found themselves, he made an attack on the Burmese encampment before Lat Ya.[60] However, the Burmese put up very strong resistance to the Thai, so that the latter were not able to take the camp in the first attack.[61] It appears that at first the Thai troops were not distinguished for their bravery. It is reported[62] that the Maha Uparat had great mortars set up and proclaimed among the soldiers and officers that whoever should flee during the battle would be pounded in the mortar.

The Burmese constructed fortified towers in which they mounted cannon with which they bombarded the camp of the Thai.[63] Thereupon the Maha Uparat procured cannon made in the Thonburi epoch and bombarded the Burmese encampment in the same way.[64] Finally the Burmese attacked.[65] It appears that for some length of time the battle remained undecided.

[59] *P.P.R.I*, p. 114; *P.P.*, p. 243. Damrong, *Thai rop Phama*, vol. 2, p. 178, locates the army of Bodawpaya "at the end of the river Lon Si."

[60] Exact statements about the battle units in this and the following battles have not come down to us, but these were determined on the basis of certain rigid schemata which were set up in accordance with the evaluation of certain facts of astrological significance; for detailed information on this see *Phichai songkhram Thai*, and Quaritch-Wales, *Ancient South-East Asian Warfare*.

[61] Damrong, *Thai rop Phama*, vol. 2, p. 178; *P.P.*, p. 243; *P.P.R.I*, p. 115. According to Phraison Salarak, *op. cit.*, p. 16, at first the Burmese attacked the Thai, but without success.

[62] *P.P.*, p. 243.

[63] Symes, *op. cit.*, vol. 1, pp. 264 *et seq.*, according to which the entire Burmese artillery at that time consisted of twenty-one howitzers that were simply worthless ship cannons which had been dismantled.

[64] According to Thai records a great many Burmese perished as a result of this; see *P.P.R.I*, p. 117, and *P.P.*, p. 245, but nothing is said of Thai losses.

[65] Damrong, *Thai rop Phama*, vol. 2, p. 177, quotes the Burmese chronicle: "The Burmese first began the battle with the Mǫn troops, which had survived from Kram Chang. The Mǫn troops fled. Then the Burmese advanced against the fortified camp of the Thai. The battle was fought according to all the rules of the art of war, but the Burmese advanced thoughtlessly with the consequence that the Thai were able to encircle a unit. When the Burmese

Meanwhile, the Maha Uparat had formed "robber troops"[66] under the command of Phraya Siharatdetchothai, Phraya Thainam and the governor of Phetburi, among others. They were to be stationed in hiding, 500 men strong, along the supply routes of the Burmese. The troops set forth but did not carry out the orders which had been given to them. They sent a few Burmese prisoners to the camp of the Maha Uparat but at the same time hid themselves in the forests. Therefore, the Maha Uparat had the three commanders, who were accused of cowardice by their own officers, seized and beheaded. The heads of the executed commanders were impaled on stakes before the camp.[67] Phra Ong Čau Khun Nen with greater forces was then commissioned to interfere with the Burmese supplies.[68] This detachment lay in ambush at Phatakhrai on a river course in the vicinity of Saiyok and was able to intercept a considerable number of supply transports. The Burmese constantly suffered serious losses. The troops under Phra Ǫng Čau Khun Nen succeeded in overwhelming a supply column with sixty elephants and in slaughtering its escort.[69]

The supply situation of the Burmese began to become critical.[70] Rama I advanced over Kančanaburi[71] toward Lat Ya with the reserve army which had been waiting in Bangkok in a state of readiness, for he believed that the troops of the Maha Uparat were too weak to undertake a really decisive battle against the Burmese.[72] In the council of war following his arrival, the Maha Uparat expressed the belief that because of their difficult supply situation the Burmese were suffering from hunger and consequently their fighting power was considerably diminished. The coming of the reserve army was not necessary. Even

commander saw that the Thai were fighting with great strength and eagerness, he regretted having allowed the battle to begin and his only hope was that he would be able to hold out." In the translation of the *Glass Palace Chronicle* by Phraison Salarak this passage is not to be found.

[66] *Kǫng čon*, in modern terminology "partisans."

[67] *P.P.*, p. 244.

[68] According to *P.P.*, p. 245: 1,000 men; according to Damrong, *Thai rop Phama*, vol. 2, p. 179: 1,800 men.

[69] *P.P.R.I*, pp. 116, 117; Damrong, *Thai rop Phama*, vol. 2, p. 179, referring to the Burmese chronicle; compare Phraison Salarak, *op. cit.*, p. 16.

[70] *Phongsawadan Mǫn Phama*, p. 381. Phayre, *op. cit.*, p. 217, says that thousands (of Burmese) died of hunger, and that the Burmese officer in charge of foraging, Meng Syo, was put to death because of his negligence in this matter.

[71] In *P.P.R.I*, pp. 117 *et seq.*, and in *P.P.*, pp. 245 *et seq.*, the reception of the king in Kančanaburi is described in detail. Despite the serious war situation Rama I was greeted by the Maha Uparat with all ceremony.

[72] *P.P.R.I*, p. 117; *P.P.*, p. 247.

without it the Burmese vanguard would soon be destroyed. The Maha Uparat proposed that the reserve army under the king should be moved to another theater of war.[73] The king agreed and returned from Kančanaburi to Bangkok by ship.[74]

At the beginning of the third lunar month of 1785 the Maha Uparat ordered his troops to attack the Burmese encampments at Lat Ya. Previously he had attempted to further the demoralization of the Burmese, already in a famished condition,[75] by having a certain number of his troops withdraw several times, unseen by the enemy, and then return in the morning with raised banners. In this way he wanted to give the Burmese the impression that new troops of his were constantly arriving.[76]

By the evening of the day of the attack the Burmese encampments were conquered.[77] The fleeing troops were pursued up to Tha Din Daeng and Sam Sop. Large quantities of booty fell into the hands of the Thai.[78] Upon receiving news of the destruction of his advance guard Bodawpaya ordered the hasty retreat of the entire main force to Martaban.[79] We have a contemporary report[80] of the almost complete disbandment of the Burmese army at that time. According to this report, Bodawpaya, upon reaching the frontier, was suddenly seized with panic because of a rumor that the king of Thailand was attacking with

[73] *P.P.R.I*, p. 119; Damrong, *Thai rop Phama*, vol. 2, p. 179. The question must remain open whether at this time the further strategy of the campaign was already decided upon, that is to say, that the king with the reserve army should advance to the north and the Maha Uparat to the south; but it seems probable that it was the outcome of the battles of Lat Ya that played a decisive role in this decision.

[74] But this does not agree with Chakrabongse, *op. cit.*, p. 99, according to which the army of the king participated in the battles of Lat Ya. This, however, cannot be established from Thai records.

[75] Damrong, *Thai rop Phama*, vol. 2, p. 180, quotes here again the Burmese chronicle. The Burmese troops fighting against the Thai suffered greatly from hunger. They had to nourish themselves with coconuts and tree roots. Domestic animals were slaughtered for food. Many Burmese were sick and died of hunger; compare Phraison Salarak, *op. cit.*, pp. 16 *et seq.*

[76] *P.P.R.I*, p. 120.

[77] At that time according to *P.P.*, pp. 249–50, a great many Burmese soldiers were killed and taken prisoner. Damrong, *Thai rop Phama*, vol. 2, p. 180, quotes again the Burmese chronicle as giving 6,000 as the correct figure. See Phraison Salarak, *op. cit.*, p. 17.

[78] According to Symes, *op. cit.*, vol. 1, p. 265, the entire Burmese artillery also.

[79] *Phongsawadan Mǫn Phama*, p. 381; *P.P.R.I*, *op. cit.*, p. 122; *P.P.*, p. 250; but according to Phraison Salarak, *op. cit.*, p. 17, the principal reason for the retreat was the famished condition of the Burmese army.

[80] Sangermano, *op. cit.*, p. 59. The author lived in Burma from 1785 to 1788. Similar statements also in Harvey, *op. cit.*, p. 271, Symes, *op. cit.*, p. 265, and Phayre, *op. cit.*, p. 217.

a large army. It was the consensus of opinion of his officers that, in view of his superiority in numbers, he could easily have overwhelmed the enemy. However, he paid no attention to all the advice given him and fled in great haste, leaving behind his elephants, his weapons and his provisions. It was not until his arrival in Rangoon that he again could feel that he was safe. At that time the peaceful attitude of the Thai king was the only thing that saved Burma from total subjugation. But this may be doubted because the Thai army at that time was by far inferior in numbers to the Burmese army; and, besides, the raids of the Thai into Burma were never very successful except those of King Naresuon in the sixteenth century.

At the same time Anǫkfaekkhitwunyi, with the main force, had set out from Thavoi with an advance guard of 3,000 men under the governor of Thavoi,[81] with a main body of 4,000 troops under Anǫkfaekkhitwunyi himself and with a rear guard of 3,000 men under Čiksinbo.[82] The route of this army was much more difficult than that of the main army over the Pass of the Three Pagodas, and the onward march was correspondingly slow. However, the advance guard finally succeeded in crossing over the mountains and in building a fortified camp at Khau Ngu in the province of Ratburi. Anǫkfaekkhitwunyi and Čiksinbo followed with their troops and settled down in encampments at Thǫng Chatri and on the right bank of the Phachi.

Anǫkfaekkhitwunyi did not yet know anything of the defeat of the main army at Lat Ya. But Phraya Thammathibǫdi and the Phraya Yomarat had also been inattentive to what was going on and had failed to observe with care the movements of the army of Anǫkfaekkhitwunyi. They therefore knew nothing of the Burmese encampments at Khau Ngu and at the Phachi.[83]

Meanwhile, after the victory of Lat Ya, the Phraya Kalahom and Phraya Saenyakǫn, conforming to the orders of the Maha Uparat, were on their way to Ratburi with part of the Maha Uparat's army.[84] In the course of their march they came upon the Burmese camp at Khau Ngu.[85] The Thai troops attacked immediately. After heavy fighting involving the use of artillery on both sides the Burmese camp was taken. The troops of the governor of Thavoi fled in a state of complete

[81] Obviously with his own troops, that means with Mǫn troops; compare footnote 56 of this chapter.

[82] *P.P.*, p. 251; in Damrong, *Thai rop Phama*, vol. 2, p. 181, referred to as Čiksibo.

[83] *P.P.R.I*, p. 123; *P.P.*, p. 251; Damrong, *Thai rop Phama*, vol. 2, p. 181.

[84] We do not know in what strength.

[85] *Phongsawadan Mǫn Phama*, p. 381.

disarray. Also, the rest of the army under Anǫkfaekkhitwunyi did not offer further resistance.[86]

The two Thai commanders sent news of the victory and of the booty to Bangkok and continued on their way to Ratburi. They also sent news to the Maha Uparat. In the letter to the king they told about the negligence of the Phraya Thammathibǫdi and the Phraya Yomarat who at that time were both in the camp at Ratburi, and they asked permission to inflict the death penalty on the two generals. Phraya Thammathibǫdi and Phraya Yomarat, however, were in Rama I's favor; and the latter therefore ordered that they should not be put to death but should both be publicly punished in another way. Thereupon the Maha Uparat had three stripes shaved on their heads and deprived them of their offices. All the remaining officers were condemned to the punishment of being cudgelled.[87]

The Ratburi army was led back to Bangkok. And the Maha Uparat set out in this direction[88] with part of his troops, while the remaining went to Ratburi.

The struggle against the Burmese northern army. The battle of Pak Nam Phing

The Burmese northern army, setting out at approximately the same time as the other armies, departed from Chiengsaen in the direction of Chiengmai.[89] An advance guard of 5,000 men under Nemayosihapati advanced over Čaehom in order to take Sawannkhalok, Sukhothai, Phitsanulok and Phichai. Chiengmai was still in a state of utter devastation as a result of the Burmese attack of 1776.[90] Therefore, Sadomahasiriutčana with 15,000 men[91] decided to attack Lampang,[92]

[86] During the flight and pursuit by the Thai troops a great number of Burmese were killed or taken prisoner, as alleged in *P.P.R.I*, p. 123; no further details are given in the Burmese chronicle as translated by Phraison Salarak, *op. cit.*, p. 18.

[87] *P.P.R.I*, p. 124.

[88] *P.P.*, p. 254; *P.P.R.I*, p. 125.

[89] The exact time of the departure cannot be ascertained, but according to *P.P.R.I*, p. 128, the siege of Lampang by the Prince of Tong U began in the first lunar month so that the departure from Chiengsaen must have been around the same time as that of the main force.

[90] The population had fled to Sawannkhalok under their governor Phraya Wichien, but was later settled in Lampang under the very able Phraya Kawila, *P.P.R.I*, p. 128.

[91] According to Prachakitčakǫračak, *Phongsawadan Yonok*, p. 488, Maengki was the commander of the Burmese forces and the siege of Lampang took place in the year 1784 (2327); Prachakitčakǫračak gives 40,000 as the number of the Burmese troops, a figure which appears to be rather too high.

[92] Concerning settlements in Lampang dating from before this siege see Prachakitčakǫračak, *op. cit.*, p. 486.

which was skillfully defended by Phraya Kawila, a very efficient and experienced warrior. Despite repeated attacks and the overwhelmingly superior force of the besieging troops,[93] Kawila succeeded in holding out for several months[94] until the arrival of replacements from Bangkok.[95] The governor also managed to get a messenger to Bangkok out of the beleaguered city with a request for help.[96] However, the remaining cities in the north, Sawannkhalok, Sukhothai, Phitsanulok, Phrae and Thoen, quickly succumbed to the superior forces of the Burmese under Nemayosihapati. Those inhabitants who could not flee were abducted.[97] That was the usual fate shared on both sides by the population of the hostile powers.

The army of Čokhongnaratha advanced along the Mae Nam Lamau to Tak without encountering any obstacles, and the city surrendered without putting up a fight.[98] The governor and the population were carried off to Burma. Čokhongnaratha and his troops entrenched themselves in the vicinity of Tak,[99] and Nemayosihapati, coming from Sawannkhalok, encamped to the south of Phitsanulok in the village of Pak Nam Phing where the Mae Nam Yom and the Mae Nam Nan[100] flow together.

The advance guard of the Thai northern army under the Phraya Mahasena had settled at Pichit, about 150 km. from Tak, where it constructed a fortified camp. The main force of the army under Krom Luong Phraratcha Wang Lang drew itself up at Nakhọn Sawann and the rear guard under the Phraya Phra Khlang and Phraya Uthaithamm at Chainat, in order to intercept any enemy troops which might approach from Uthaithani.[101]

[93] Prachakitčakọračak, *op. cit.*, p. 488, states that the strength of the troops defending Lampang was 1,000 men, a figure which seems reasonable in view of the size of the cities of northern Thailand at that time.

[94] According to *Phongsawadan Mọn Phama*, p. 382, and *P.P.R.I*, p. 132, four months; according to Prachakitčakọračak, *op. cit.*, p. 489, two months and twenty-six days. Damrong, *Thai rop Phama*, vol. 2, p. 186, is inclined to accept the former statement, the besieging troops allegedly withdrew in the fifth lunar month. No details of the siege of Lampang are given in Phraison Salarak, *op. cit.*, p. 18.

[95] References cited in footnote 94 and Damrong, *Thai rop Phama*, vol. 2, p. 185; Mahāamatayathibọdi, *Phongsawadan Chiengmai*, p. 77.

[96] *Phongsawadan Mọn Phama*, p. 382.

[97] Prachakitčakọračak, *op. cit.*, p. 488; compare Phraison Salarak, *op. cit.*, p. 17.

[98] Damrong, *Thai rop Phama*, vol. 2, p. 182, with reference to the Burmese chronicle. See Phraison Salarak, *op. cit.*, p. 17.

[99] *P.P.*, p. 256, but according to this source Chuithọngweračọnaeng was the commander.

[100] According to Damrong, *Thai rop Phama*, vol. 2, p. 183, the Mae Nam Yai, but he probably means the Nan river.

[101] *P.P.R.I*, p. 114; *P.P.*, p. 242.

The two sides remained poised in an expectant state, for neither felt strong enough to undertake a decisive battle. However, the strategy of Bangkok revealed itself to the extent that the relatively weak forces of the Phraratcha Wang Lang were able to hold up the further advance of the Burmese northern army in the direction of Bangkok, although at the same time the outcome of the struggle against the Burmese main forces had not yet been decided.

After the battle of Lat Ya, Rama I, with the reserve army of 30,000[102] men under his command, hastened north in the direction of Inthaburi, where he constructed a fortified camp.[103] From here he commanded the Krom Phraratcha Wang Lang, on pain of death,[104] to join together in forced marches with the troops of the Phraya Mahasena and to attack the Burmese at Pak Nam Phing.[105] The king also commanded Krom Luong Thepharirak to join the troops of the Phraya Phra Khlang and Phraya Uthaithamm immediately at Chainat, where they were to attack the Burmese encamped at Rahaeng.[106] Meanwhile, the king himself marched with his troops as far as Nakhǫn Sawann in order to join up with the army of the Phraratcha Wang Lang.[107]

At dawn on the fourth day of the fourth lunar month 2328, *i.e.*, the beginning of March, 1785, Phraya Mahasena attacked the Burmese encampment at Pak Nam Phing.[108] The advance guard was under the command of the governor of Saraburi. Phraya Mahasena himself commanded the main force. The Krom Phraratcha Wang Lang followed immediately behind.

[102] *P.P.R.I*, p. 127; *P.P.*, p. 255; Damrong, *Thai rop Phama*, vol. 2, p. 134.

[103] According to *P.P.R.I*, p. 125, and *P.P.*, p. 254, the departure of Rama I had been preceded by a conference in Bangkok with the Maha Uparat at which the strategy for the remainder of this campaign was fixed. Compare footnote 73 of this chapter. See also *Phongsawadan Mǫn Phama*, p. 381.

[104] *P.P.*, p. 255.

[105] This is Damrong's account, *Thai rop Phama*, vol. 2, p. 184, but according to *P.P.R.I*, *op. cit.*, pp. 128 *et seq.*, and *P.P.*, p. 254, only the troops of the Phraya Mahasena were to attack at Pak Nam Phing. It is, however, highly improbable that the troops of the Phraratcha Wang Lang were expected to remain idle at Nakhǫn Sawann in the meantime. One possibility which cannot be excluded is that Mahasena was *at first*, that is to say, immediately after receiving the command of the Phraratcha Wang Lang, to attack the Burmese alone in the certainty that the Phraratcha Wang Lang would immediately follow with reinforcements. The latter through this command and execution may have hoped to avoid the threatened death penalty; see *P.P.*, pp. 257, 258, and *P.P.R.I*, pp. 129, 130.

[106] *P.P.R.I*, pp. 128 *et seq.*

[107] Damrong, *Thai rop Phama*, vol. 2, p. 185; *P.P.*, p. 258; *P.P.R.I*, p. 130.

[108] Compare footnote 105 of this chapter. No details of this battle are to be found in the Burmese chronicle according to Phraison Salarak, *op. cit.*, pp. 17 *et seq.*

The advance guard of the Phraya Saraburi arrived at the east bank of the river, behind which the Burmese were stationed.[109] In the dawn movements in the river bed were vaguely perceived. The governor of Saraburi was a cautious and timorous man; and, under the impression that the Burmese were crossing the river, he ordered a hasty retreat. However, by daylight it became apparent that the river was inhabited by a flock of pelicans[110] and that it was simply from this flock that the Thai advance guard had retreated. The Phraya Saraburi was beheaded.[111]

After a violent struggle the Burmese encampment was taken in the evening. The Burmese had been careless in their choice of location for the camp. The rear of the camp was enclosed by flowing waters which the Burmese had to pass in order to escape. Consequently, many of them were drowned.[112]

When Rama I received the news of victory he detached a part of his main force, placed under the command of the Krom Luong Čakaračetsada, and ordered these troops to unite with those of the Phraya Mahasena and then pursue and annihilate the Burmese. The besieging troops at Lampang were defeated in the first attack. From his position inside the city Phraya Kawila gave his support to the struggle. The Burmese army, reinforced by the troops of Nemayosihapati defeated at Pak Nam Phing, were routed and fled to Chiengsaen.[113]

After these events took place the main body of the Thai northern army returned to Bangkok. A number of further fights of a purely local nature occurred around Chiengsaen. They were carried out by the governors of Nan and Phrae and by the minor Lao rulers nearby. Ultimately the Burmese were also expelled from Chiengsaen.[114]

Rama I had returned to Nakhǫn Sawann with the remaining part of the main force which he still led. The Krom Phraratcha Wang Lang also returned there with his troops in order to guard the Burmese prisoners.

The Burmese army stationed at Rahaeng under the command of Čokhongnaratha no longer engaged in battle after the retreat of Bod-

[109] From the references given it is not clear which is the river in question.

[110] *Nok krathung.*

[111] *P.P.R.I*, p. 129.

[112] According to *P.P.*, p. 259, and *P.P.R.I*, p. 130, at least 800 Burmese. See also *Khamhaikan chau angwa*, p. 22.

[113] Probably in the fifth lunar month of 2328. See footnote 94 of this chapter.

[114] Suriyapong, *Phongsawadan Nan*, pp. 126 *et seq.;* Prachakitčakǫračak, *op. cit.*, p. 490.

awpaya and after the defeat at Pak Nam Phing had become known. When the Thai troops under Krom Luong Thepharirak and Phraya Uthaithamm pushed forward to Kamphaengphet, the Burmese withdrew along the Mae Nam Lamau.[115]

Thereupon the king ordered the return of all troops to Nakhǫn Sawann and from there to Bangkok. At the conclusion of the northern campaign various persons were promoted to a higher rank[116] and an amnesty was granted to officers who had been under punishment.

Conflict on the Malayan Peninsula, 1785

Since the beginning of hostilities in the first lunar month, 2328 (December, 1784) the Burmese southern army had occupied almost the whole of southern Thailand which was virtually defenseless. Mergui was the rallying point of the army of Kaengwunmaengyi.[117]

From this point a naval detachment of 3,000 men under Yiwun proceeded to Thalang. Kaengwunmaengyi, with 7,000 men including an advance guard of 2,500 under Nemayokhungnarat and a main force of 4,500, proceeded by land to Chumphǫn by way of Kraburi, Ranong and Bakčan. In Chumphǫn there were only very weak defensive forces. The population fled into the surrounding jungles and the city was pillaged and set on fire.[118] Chaiya was taken under the same circumstances.

On the other hand, the governor Phat of Nakhǫn Si Thammarat had prepared for the defense of the city[119] even though he was aware of the fact that Chumphǫn and Chaiya had already fallen. He assembled a small detachment of around 1,000 men whose task it was to bar a river course before the way of the Burmese to Nakhǫn Si Thammarat. Thereupon the Burmese officers had Thai prisoners from Chaiya cry out that Bangkok had already fallen, and that Nakhǫn Si Thammarat should surrender or otherwise the city would be razed to the ground. Phraya Phat was in total ignorance of the military situation in other

[115] *P.P.R.I*, p. 132; Damrong, *Thai rop Phama*, vol. 2, p. 185.

[116] Among other promotions at this time the Krom Luong Phraratcha Wang Lang was elevated to the rank Krom Phra, *P.P.*, p. 262.

[117] *P.P.R.I*, p. 134; *P.P.*, p. 262.

[118] *P.P.*, p. 263. See also the very short account of the conflict in southern Thailand in the Burmese chronicle according to Phraison Salarak, *op. cit.*, pp. 18 *et seq.*

[119] Anusǫnsithikham, *Phongsawadan Nakhǫn Si Thammarat*, p. 108, and in Si Wǫrawat, *Phongsawadan Pathalung*, p. 31, further statements about the history of the Phraya Phat.

theaters of war; he only knew that all the principal cities of South Thailand had already been destroyed before Nakhọn Si Thammarat and that no assistance had come from Bangkok. Furthermore, his defensive troops were greatly inferior in numbers to those of the Burmese. He therefore abandoned all resistance and fled to the mountains to the west of the city; most of the inhabitants did likewise. Nakhọn Si Thammarat was occupied and plundered[120] by the Burmese army without a struggle. Male inhabitants who did not flee were killed, and women and children were carried off as prisoners.[121] The Burmese southern army continued on its way to Pathalung and Songkhla.[122]

The detachment under Yiwun had taken Takuapa and was preparing to lay siege to Thalang. Just before the arrival of the Burmese the governor died and a new appointment to replace him had not yet been made. The resistance therefore came under the direction of the widow of the deceased, Khun Ying Čan, who was descended from the old nobility of Thalang, and her sister, Nang Muk, together with the officials of the city.[123] With the help of the entire population Thalang was skillfully defended; even women participated in the struggle. Consequently, the Burmese could not take the city and were obliged to withdraw because of insufficient nourishment.[124]

Immediately after the struggle against the Burmese main force had come to an end, the Maha Uparat departed to the south, arriving at Chumphọn by ship around the time of the fourth lunar month 1785.[125] He believed that with approximately 20,000 men[126] he would be able to drive the Burmese out of South Thailand.[127] When he arrived in Chumphọn he ordered the Phraya Kalahom and Phraya Saenyakọn to move to Chaiya. Meanwhile, all Burmese forces had assembled at Nakhọn Si Thammarat and were advancing in the direction of Pathalung. The population of this city fled when they received news of the Burmese

[120] Damrong, *Thai rop Phama,* vol. 2, p. 188, quotes the Burmese chronicle according to which the transport ship with the stolen goods from Nakhọn Si Thammarat went down in a storm.

[121] *P.P.*, p. 265.

[122] Anusọnsithikham, *op. cit.*, p. 108.

[123] Anusọnsithikham, *op. cit.*, p. 110; *P.P.R.I,* p. 137; Harvey, *op. cit.*, p. 271.

[124] See also Symes, *op. cit.*, vol. 1, pp. 261 *et seq.*, 264.

[125] *P.P.R.I,* p. 125; *Phongsawadan Mọn Phama*, p. 381; *P.P.*, p. 254.

[126] *P.P.R.I,* p. 138; *P.P.*, p. 267.

[127] A description of this campaign in poetry is to be found in the *Nirat sadet pai prap Phama müang Nakhọn Si Thammarat 2329,* which was composed by the Maha Uparat himself. However, this work does not reveal new historical facts.

approach. However, a monk, Phra Mahachui, who was believed by the population to have magical powers at his disposal, managed to persuade the governor, Phraya Khaenkorop,[128] and the inhabitants to offer resistance and to defend the city.[129] Magical charms and cloths were produced and distributed. A small force of a thousand soldiers was put together. The Phra Mahachui was carried on a stretcher before the city where the defensive force had drawn itself up. However, no battle took place, probably because the Burmese had learned of the arrival of the Maha Uparat and therefore had not advanced farther to the south.[130]

Kaengwunmaengyi commanded Nemayokhungnarat to put himself at the head of the advance guard against the Thai forces. He himself followed with the main force in a northerly direction. At Chaiya the advance guard met the first Thai troops. The Burmese hastily attempted to set up a fortified camp, but they were encircled and hard pressed by the Thai troops. There was heavy rain on this day so that neither side could use cannon. In the evening the Burmese began to flee from the provisional camp which they had erected.[131] The pursuit continued into the night. The troops of Kaengwunmaengyi, following from Nakhǫn Si Thammarat, no longer engaged in battle after receiving news of the defeat of the advance guard but fled across the peninsula to Kraburi and from there to Burma. With this event the struggle on the Malayan peninsula came to an end in 1785.

The governor of Nakhǫn Si Thammarat and the governor of Phathalung were reappointed to their offices. In the investigation carried out by the Maha Uparat it became clear that the Burmese had had such an immensely superior force that there had been no real possibility of defending the cities.[132] Moreover, for many months the governors had no news about the situation in other localities where fighting had been going on. Nevertheless, the Maha Uparat expressly declared that in the future all cities should be defended exactly as in the past.[133]

[128] Si Wǫrawat, *op. cit.*, p. 32, gives the name of the governor as Khang Lek.

[129] Anusǫnsithikham, *op. cit.*, p. 109; *P.P.*, pp. 266 *et seq.*

[130] *P.P.R.I*, p. 267; Damrong, *Thai rop Phama*, vol. 2, p. 189. According to Anusǫnsithikham, *op. cit.*, p. 109, the Burmese fled with terror at the sight of Phathalung's forces.

[131] *Phongsawadan Mǫn Phama*, p. 382; Anusǫnsithikham, *op. cit.*, p. 109; Damrong, *Thai rop Phama*, vol. 2, p. 190.

[132] Wichienkhiri, *Phongsawadan Songkhla II*, p. 10.

[133] *P.P.R.I*, p. 139; *P.P.*, p. 269.

Other officers who had particularly distinguished themselves in battle were elevated in rank.[134]

From Nakhǫn Si Thammarat the Maha Uparat led his troops further to the south in order to bring the northern Malayan sultanates once again under the jurisdiction of Bangkok.[135]

The second Burmese invasion of 1786. The battles at Tha Din Daeng and Sam Sop

Discontented as he naturally was about the fiasco of 1785, Bodawpaya decided only one year later to make a new attack on Thailand. All armies, particularly the northern and southern ones,[136] had suffered great losses because of death, wounds and captivity. At the three rallying points, Ava, Martaban and Thavoi, the armies were reorganized and prepared for battle.

Bodawpaya had obviously come to recognize the error of his strategy of the previous year and now decided to push forward to Bangkok over the Pass of the Three Pagodas, the shortest route, with only one army.[137]

Bodawpaya commissioned Kaken to set up supply camps in the entire Mǫn territory. Ample supplies of rice were also on hand in Martaban. At the end of the rainy season the entire army was concentrated together. Insae, the first son of Bodawpaya, led the main force[138] with 50,000 men;[139] Bodawpaya followed with a second army.[140]

Insae set out from Martaban in the twelfth lunar month, *i.e.*, about December, 1785.[141] Mienwun and Mienmewun went before him with

[134] See Anusǫnsithikham, *op. cit.*, p. 111, and *P.P.*, p. 273. Among others the Khun Ying Čan was elevated to the rank Thau Thep Kasatri, Nang Muk to Thau Si Sunthǫn. The abbot Phra Mahachui was nominated Phraya Thukkharat of Phathalung, according to Si Wǫrawat, *op. cit.*, p. 32; see also *P.P.*, p. 269.

[135] *Phongsawadan Mǫn Phama*, p. 382; *P.P.R.I*, p. 138. See p. 101.

[136] *P.P.R.I*, p. 152. Compare Launay, *Histoire de la Mission de Siam 1662–1811*, vol. 2, p. 321.

[137] *P.P.*, p. 274.

[138] This is definitely stated only in *Phongsawadan Mǫn Phama*, p. 382. Compare Damrong, *Thai rop Phama*, vol. 2, p. 197. In Phraison Salarak, *op. cit.*, p. 20, Mingyi Nanda Kyawadin is named as supreme commander of this army.

[139] According to *P.P.R.I*, p. 152; *P.P.*, p. 274; Damrong, *Thai rop Phama*, vol. 2, p. 194. According to Phraison Salarak, *op. cit.*, p. 20: 55,000 men.

[140] Concerning which we have no further information in any of the known records.

[141] In a *klǫn phleng yau* poem the drawing up of the armies and the battles are depicted in poetic forms, *Nirat rop Phama thi Tha Din Daeng* composed by Rama I. Literary and historical comment on this poem is to be found in *Prawat wannakhadi Thai*, p. 267.

30,000 men, having been charged with the task of constructing fortified camps on Thai territory for the armies following them. They also had the task of seeing that the necessary supplies were on hand. At the same time, they received orders not to become engaged in battle under any circumstances while crossing over the mountains.

The advance army succeeded in reaching the plain and constructed big camps with trenches and ramparts at Tha Din Daeng and Sam Sop.[142] The location of the camps was so well chosen and the fortifications were so skillfully laid out that the Thai were at first deprived of all possibility of making a successful attack. The Burmese gathered supplies in large quantities, which they obtained from the surrounding territory. The routes by which the armies following from behind were approaching were provided with bridges when necessary. Insae established an additional encampment in the vicinity of the Pass of the Three Pagodas at Mae Kasat, that is to say, where the main force under Bodawpaya would necessarily follow. There he awaited news of the advance army.

Spies from Kančanaburi, Siwat and Saiyok informed the Thai government about Burmese troop movements and encampments. The decision was made not to allow the Burmese to come again as far as Lat Ya but to engage them in battle farther to the north.

An advance army of 30,000 men led by the Maha Uparat and the Phraya Ratanaphiphit set out in February[143] in the direction of Saiyok. An army of equal strength under the leadership of the Krom Phraratcha Wang Lang followed.[144] Both armies reached Saiyok going up the Mae Nam Saiyok by ship. At this point the army of the Maha Uparat was divided into separate detachments. Three detachments under Ratanaphiphit, Phraya Kalahom and Phraya Saenyakǫn totaling 20,000 men and a fourth with 10,000 soldiers under the Maha Uparat marched in the direction of Sam Sop with a view to attacking the Burmese encampments which were situated there.[145]

The second army under the Phraratcha Wang Lang and the king

[142] *P.P.*, p. 275; *P.P.R.I*, p. 153; Sonakun, *op. cit.*, pp. 24 *et seq.* According to Launay, *Histoire de la Mission de Siam 1662–1811*, vol. 2, p. 321, the Burmese had reached Thai territory by around February, 1786.

[143] The exact time of the departure and the corresponding astrological viewpoint is given in *Čotmaihet hon*, p. 10. Launay, *Histoire de la Mission de Siam 1662–1811*, vol. 2, p. 321, figures out that the strength of the Thai army was 90,000 soldiers.

[144] The king was probably also with this army.

[145] *P.P.R.I*, p. 155; *P.P.*, p. 277.

advanced from Saiyok to Tha Khanum and encamped at Tha Din Daeng, about two kilometers from the camp of the Burmese. After the Maha Uparat once again united his forces with the three advance detachments, the two armies, that of the Maha Uparat and that of the king, advanced to attack the enemy at Tha Din Daeng and at Sam Sop on the fifth day of the fourth lunar month (the beginning of March). For three days there was heavy fighting involving the use of cannon on both sides. Around noon on Friday, the seventh day of the month, the Thai forces penetrated into the Burmese encampments. The Burmese continued to resist until evening when they fled before the superior force of the enemy. The Thai forces continued the pursuit up to the camp of Insae at Mae Kasat. The latter was unable to stop the general disintegration[146] and had to retreat with his forces to Martaban in disorder.[147] Both in battle and in flight the Burmese suffered heavy losses through death and captivity. Moreover, a great deal of booty, elephants, weapons and supplies of all kinds fell into the hands of the victors.[148] Thailand had won a decisive battle. Within a month of the departure from Bangkok the second Burmese war under Rama I came to an end.

The third Burmese war, 1787. The struggle in northern Thailand

After the second defeat of the Burmese in 1786 the decision was made in Bangkok that Burma should now be invaded[149] with a larger army.[150] However, the Thai troops had not yet set out when news was received of the Burmese invasion of North Thailand. The army was then divided into two parts. The Maha Uparat went north with the

[146] But according to *P.P.R.I*, p. 156, Insae did attempt to offer resistance to the Thai. Damrong, *Thai rop Phama*, vol. 2, p. 196, is probably in agreement with this opinion.

[147] Damrong, *Thai rop Phama*, vol. 2, p. 197, refers once again to Sangermano, *op. cit.*, but the latter's remarks probably relate to the year 1785.

[148] Damrong, *Thai rop Phama*, vol. 2, p. 196, with regard to this matter quotes the Burmese chronicle in which the great Burmese losses in men and animals were explicitly stated, but such statements are not to be found in the translation of this chronicle by Phraison Salarak, *op. cit.*, p. 21; according to Launay, *Histoire de la Mission de Siam, 1662–1811*, vol. 2, p. 321, the struggle came to an end "without any great massacre," but in making this statement Launay is apparently thinking of the Thai troops.

[149] *P.P.*, p. 283; Symes, *op. cit.*, vol. 1, p. 264.

[150] Damrong, *Thai rop Phama*, vol. 2, p. 206, gives the number of 80,000 soldiers. His statement is apparently based on the Burmese chronicle (Phraison Salarak, *op. cit.*, p. 32), but in a footnote Damrong questions this statement and expresses the opinion that not more than 50,000 men were involved.

larger part,[151] and the king departed for Thavoi with the remaining troops[152] at the beginning of January, 1787, on the fifth day of the second lunar month.

The victories of Thailand in 1785 and 1786 caused various reactions in Burma, a country consisting of many different peoples. In particular, it appears that after the defeats of Bodawpaya the Shan around Chiengtung and Chiengrung again became restive and that military force was needed in order to subjugate them once again.[153] Relevant to this situation, Čokhongnaratha with 5,000 men was ordered to bring the cities of northern Thailand under control of Burma again. With the help of the troops from Chiengsaen, Fang and the plain north of Chiengmai were retaken.[154] After this event the Burmese troops had to reserve the rice fields around Fang for their own needs. Accounts of the other events of this campaign are so different in the various records that it is impossible to get an entirely clear picture.[155] Thus the course of the campaign can be told only in general outline. Particular events cannot be ascertained, nor is it possible to put events in proper chronological order.

While the Burmese under Čokhongnaratha were engaged in operations at Fang, Mangchai, the governor of Phrae, and the Phraya Yong lined up for the attack on Chiengsaen, the defense[156] of which was under the command of the Burmese governor, Aparakamani.[157] The city was conquered, however, and Aparakamani fled with the rest of his troops to Chiengrai. Mangchai and the Phraya Yong continued the pursuit up to that point and with the help of the governor were able to

[151] According to Damrong, *Thai rop Phama*, vol. 2, pp. 203, 206, 60,000 soldiers, but Damrong himself questions this statement (see footnote 150); he thinks that the strength of this army did not amount to more than 30,000 men.

[152] According to *P.P.*, p. 284, and Damrong, *Thai rop Phama*, vol. 2, p. 206, 20,000 men.

[153] Sonakun, *op. cit.*, p. 25; Damrong, *Thai rop Phama*, *loc. cit.*, quotes the Burmese chronicle according to which Bodawpaya dispatched the Wunyimahachaisura with 45,000 troops to put down the rebellion of the Shan. See Phraison Salarak, *op. cit.*, p. 32. Compare also Harvey, *op. cit.*, p. 271.

[154] *P.P.R.I*, p. 159; *P.P.*, p. 279; Damrong, *Thai rop Phama*, vol. 2, p. 200.

[155] Damrong, *Thai rop Phama*, vol. 2, p. 199, agrees but only with reference to the differences between the Thai and the Burmese accounts. In reality the problem is more complicated, as even the various Thai accounts differ from one another.

[156] *P.P.*, p. 279, states that Bodawpaya commanded the Aparakamani to defend the city with 3,000 men but that 2,500 of these soldiers took to flight.

[157] According to *P.P.*, p. 279, and *P.P.R.I*, p. 160. According to Damrong, *Thai rop Phama*, vol. 2, p. 200, the governor of Chiengsaen was Pomayunguon during whose time other battles at Chiengsaen are said to have already taken place before this one. Damrong, *ibid.*, remarks that at that time the city was still in a state of devastation. In other Thai records nothing is said of these battles.

get hold of Aparakamani. The latter was sent to Bangkok at the command of the governor of Lampang, Kawila. The governors of Phrae and Yong were rewarded for their services; but the Phraya Phrae, who for a long time have been under Burmese rule, was nevertheless an object of suspicion, for it was thought that his behavior might be a ruse. He, too, was therefore obliged to remain in Bangkok.[158]

Aparakamani declared that it was the intention of the Burmese to make an attack on Lampang in the next dry season and after that to rebuild and fortify Chiengmai.[159] That meant that the Burmese were making new arrangements to bring North Thailand permanently under their control. The consideration that the adjacent Shan peoples would be more easily dominated under these circumstances undoubtedly played a decisive role in this plan.

When Rama I was informed of the Burmese intentions he ordered Kawila, the governor of Lampang, plus part of the population of Lampang to settle in Chiengmai and to build up and fortify the city.[160] In Lampang the younger brother of Kawila, Khamsom, was nominated governor. For the time being, Lamphun had to remain in a state of devastation, for there were not enough people on hand to resettle it.[161] And Chiengmai itself, because of the scarcity of people, could not at first be resettled, so that Kawila eventually settled at Pasang, only a few kilometers away.

It is uncertain whether any battles took place at Chiengmai or Lampang in 1787. Thai records differ from each other and from Burmese chronicles regarding this matter. However, the detailed account of events in the *Chronicle of North Thailand*[162] is probably truthworthy. According to this account[163] a large Burmese force[164] set out from Chiengtung in the direction of Chiengmai. This force was

[158] *P.P.R.I*, p. 161.

[159] *P.P.*, p. 281. According to *P.P.R.I*, p. 162, the Phraya Kawila was responsible for conveying this news to Bangkok. Sonakun, *op. cit.*, p. 25, gives no definite information on this point.

[160] *P.P.R.I*, pp. 162 *et seq.*; Damrong, *Thai rop Phama*, vol. 2, p. 201; *P.P.*, p. 282; Prachakitčakǫračak, *op. cit.*, p. 490. According to *P.P.R.I*, *loc. cit.*, the order for the resettlement of Chiengmai came from the Maha Uparat after his arrival in northern Thailand, and Mahāamatayathibǫdi, *op. cit.*, p. 78, is of the same opinion.

[161] *P.P.R.I*, p. 163; Mahāamatayathibǫdi, *op. cit.*, p. 78.

[162] *Phongsawadan Yonok*, by Prachakitčakǫračak.

[163] *Ibid.*, p. 491, and Damrong, *Thai rop Phama*, vol. 2, pp. 202 *et seq.*, who alleges that these statements are based on the Burmese chronicle. *P.P.R.I*, pp. 162 *et seq.*, gives a different account. *P.P.* contains no statements on this matter.

[164] We have no statements concerning the strength of these troops, but in Prachakitčakǫračak, *op. cit.*, p. 491, Asaewunki, who was always in charge of large forces, is said to have been the commander-in-chief. According to Damrong, *Thai rop Phama*, vol. 2, p. 202, Wunyimahachaisura was the commander-in-chief.

united at Fang with the troops stationed there under Čokhongnaratha, and a battle took place[165] with the Thai provincial troops[166] from Kamphaengphet and Nakhǫn Sawann. But it appears that the Thai troops were unsuccessful and that they were not able to force back the Burmese army. An attempt was therefore made to defend the fortified points of the country with particular attention to Lampang, where the population of the other cities in the north had fled.[167]

Meanwhile Bodawpaya from Martaban sent off another army of 35,000 men under Letalasihasing; this army was to take Pasang.[168] The Burmese troops descending from the north repeatedly attacked Lampang,[169] which was skillfully defended by Khamsom. And the attempt to take Pasang, the defense of which was obviously under the command of Kawila, was equally unsuccessful despite several attacks. Finally both cities were laid under siege in the hope of starving them out.

This was the situation, more or less, when in the fourth lunar month the army of the Maha Uparat arrived before Lampang. According to the Burmese chronicle,[170] the besieging troops were encircled and completely cut off from all supplies. It was arranged with the defender in the city to attack the Burmese jointly at the same time. A four-day battle destroyed the Burmese army, the remnants of which fled to Chiengsaen.[171] The Maha Uparat then hastened to the aid of Pasang which was in a state of siege. This city was relieved in the same way. The remaining northern cities still under Burmese control were conquered by Phraya Kawila and the governor of Nan.[172]

[165] It is not clear whether the fighting took place at Lampang or at Pasang, but it was apparently at both cities, as Damrong, *Thai rop Phama*, vol. 2, p. 202, assumes. According to Prachakitčakǫračak, *op. cit.*, p. 491, there was fighting only at Pasang (Wieng Ba Chang?). But perhaps such statements refer to the sieges of Lampang and Pasang mentioned later.

[166] It cannot be ascertained who commanded the Thai troops. Damrong, *Thai rop Phama*, vol. 2, p. 202, simply remarks that the governors of Kamphaengphet and Nakhǫn Sawann hastened to the aid of Kawila at the command of Rama I, but the source of this statement by Damrong is not known. According to the *Phongsawadan Mǫn Phama*, p. 382, one may infer that the Maha Uparat was the commander, but according to Prachakitčakǫračak, *op. cit.*, p. 491, it was the Phraya Kawila.

[167] Prachakitčakǫračak, *op. cit.*, p. 491.

[168] According to Damrong, *Thai rop Phama*, vol. 2, p. 202, whose account is probably based on Burmese statements, as Thai sources say nothing about this.

[169] Damrong, *Thai rop Phama*, vol. 2, p. 202; Phraison Salarak, *op. cit.*, pp. 33 *et seq.*

[170] Quoted in Damrong, *Thai rop Phama*, p. 203, and in Phraison Salarak, *op. cit.*, p. 34.

[171] On the other hand, *P.P.R.I*, p. 162, expressly denies that there was any fighting at Lampang, "as no Burmese troops approached."

[172] Prachakitčakǫračak, *op. cit.*, pp. 492 *et seq.*

The Maha Uparat returned with his army to Bangkok. It appears that in the following years conflicts of a local character were constantly taking place but without being carried to the point of general warfare.[173]

Phraya Kawila was still unable to rebuild the devastated city of Chiengmai in depopulated North Thailand. Meanwhile, Pasang took over the position which this city had previously had.[174]

The attack of the Thai army on Thavoi, 1787

The reasons for a Thai attack on Burmese territory in the year 1787 are easy enough to understand. After the repeated Burmese invasions and the consequent great devastation, particularly in the cities, it is fairly clear that the policy of Thailand was henceforth determined by strongly emotional forces in the ruling class aiming at retaliatory measures. Since the time of Phra Narai, *i.e.*, for more than 100 years, all fighting between the two hostile states had taken place on Thai territory. The defeat of the Burmese in 1785 and 1786 provided a suitable occasion for demonstrating the national self-consciousness of the Thai and the military power which they had regained since 1767 by an attack on Burma. Though strategic considerations also played a role in the planning of the invasion,[175] they did not provide the decisive impulse. The military thinking of that age was not yet sufficiently complex. However, another consideration played an important part in the decision to attack in the direction of Thavoi in southern Burma. The majority of the inhabitants of that territory were Mǫn, some of whom, at least temporarily, did not willingly endure Burmese rule. Throughout the centuries the Mǫn had repeatedly demonstrated their desire for independence, and their efforts to achieve such independence had often been put down by bloodshed. Considerable numbers of that highly intelligent people had fled to Thailand and had settled there in various regions. Under those circumstances people in Thailand had legitimate reasons for hoping that the Mǫn, when their territory was invaded by the Thai, would at the same time rise up against Burma and in this way give their support to the attack of the Thai.

The necessary forces were lacking for a large-scale invasion which

[173] Prachakitčakǫračak, *op. cit.*, p. 493.

[174] An account of the desolate, devastated condition of Chiengmai as late as 2333 (1790) is to be found in Prachakitčakǫračak, *op. cit.*, p. 493.

[175] Damrong's interpretation, *Thai rop Phama*, vol. 2, p. 209, of the reasons for the invasion is too tendentious and is not sufficiently in agreement with the circumstances of that time.

may perhaps have been planned after the departure of the troops of the Maha Uparat northward. With the remaining relatively weak forces of the king it was clear that it would be possible to achieve only a limited military victory. The point of attack, Thavoi, was well chosen. On one hand it could be reached from central Burma only by long marches, while, on the other hand, the remaining part of southern Burma could be cut off without further difficulty from this point.

The advance guard of the invading army was led in three detachments by Phraya Ratanaphiphit, Phraya Mahasena, and by the Phraya Yomarat. These three detachments together had about 10,000 men.[176] The main force followed under the king with the Phraya Khlang as superintendent[177] and the future Rama II, Čau Fa Krom Luong Isarasunthǫn, as judge for martial affairs.[178] The rear guard was led by Krom Luong Thepharirak.[179]

About 20,000 men went up to the Mae Nam Saiyok and from this point proceeded to Tha Takua. There the army was divided into two parts, each of which was to cross over the mountains at the frontier by a different route. The southern route led over Bǫngti, the northern over the "High Mountain Pass,"[180] which terminated directly at Thavoi. This pass was the nearest route but was very difficult to walk over. The main force, which was to take Thavoi, went by this route. It was not until arrival at the point of the pass that it was observed that this route was not even suitable for foot soldiers.[181] The elephants for riding and the carrying of goods had to put their trunks around trees in order to pull themselves up the mountains. Many fell with their drivers into the ravines. Pack saddles had to be removed from the backs of all the other elephants and carried by the soldiers themselves. The king, who at that time was almost fifty years old, pulled himself up the mountains with ropes which were fastened to trees. Moreover, the descent on the Burmese side was scarcely less dangerous.

Kaengwunmaengyi, one of the Burmese commanders during the attack on Thailand in 1785, was still at Thavoi with his troops when the Thai attacked.[182] The commander in the city itself was Maengčanča,

[176] *P.P.*, p. 284.
[177] *Kiekkai.*
[178] *Nayokkrabat.*
[179] *P.P.R.I*, p. 168.
[180] Chong Khau Sung.
[181] *P.P.R.I*, p. 271; *P.P.*, p. 288.
[182] *P.P.*, pp. 285, 286; Damrong, *Thai rop Phama*, vol. 2, p. 211, with reference to the same account in the Burmese chronicle. Compare Phraison Salarak, *op. cit.*, pp. 19, 20, see also Symes, *op. cit.*, vol. 1, p. 266.

who rapidly made preparations for the defense of Thavoi. Natmilaeng, with a detachment of 3,000 men, was drawn up at Dan Wang Po at the very place where the Thai army, having crossed over the pass, would come into the plain. Another detachment took position at Kliǫng,[183] and a third of 4,000 men under the governor of Thavoi, Wun, drew itself up in the plain extending from Kliǫng to Thavoi. Kaengwunmaengyi remained in Thavoi.

The advance detachment of the Phraya Ratanaphiphit under Phraya Surasena and Phraya Mahāamat encountered the Burmese troops at Dan Wang Po on Saturday, the ninth day of the waning moon in the third lunar month. The Thai detachment first entrenched itself in an encampment opposite that of the Burmese before attacking. A violent battle took place involving the use of artillery on both sides. Phraya Surasena and other officers were killed in action.[184] The Thai troop were obliged to withdraw. One day after this fight, on the tenth day of the month, Phraya Mahasena approached. By means of a joint attack on the part of all Thai troops it was possible to take the Burmese camp on the same day. Natmilaeng withdrew with his troops in order to defend Kliǫng. Phraya Mahasena allowed his troops to have two days of rest and then continued the pursuit to Kliǫng. This city was conquered after only one day of fighting.[185] The Burmese opened the gates of the town and fled to Thavoi. The detachment of the Phraya Mahasena halted in Kliǫng, where it replenished its supplies.[186]

Meanwhile, the main army under the king had arrived at Dan Wang Po. There it was said that the Burmese had erected a fortified camp at Thǫng Thung on the way to Thavoi. Phraya Ratanaphiphit and Phraya Mahasena were asked to investigate this matter and, if the occasion should arise, to make an attack on the camp. There was heavy fighting in the course of which the Thai troops with their superior force were victorious. In the night following the day of the battle[187] the Burmese were pursued as far as Thavoi.

The defensive troops in Thavoi under Kaengwunmaengyi and Maengčanča saw the Thai troops approaching. A council of war was held at which the decision was made not to run the risk of a siege, for it

[183] According to *P.P.R.I*, p. 169, and Damrong, *op. cit.*, p. 212, 1,000 men; in *P.P.*, p. 286, "5,000 troops in another Tambon" are mentioned.

[184] *P.P.*, p. 287.

[185] *Čotmaihet hon*, p. 10; Narinthewi, *op. cit.*, p. 215.

[186] *P.P.R.I*, p. 172.

[187] That was the night after the eighth day of the waning moon of the fourth lunar month, *P.P.R.I*, p. 172.

was not clear whether or not the inhabitants of Thavoi would side with the Thai.[188] And there was the further danger that supplies might not hold out. Thavoi was evacuated. The Burmese troops crossed the river bank opposite the city.[189]

Phraya Ratanaphiphit and Phraya Mahasena marched up to Thavoi.[190] They observed that the troops had abandoned the ramparts but that the gates to the city were closed. Believing that this was simply a ruse they set up a camp outside the city by which Thavoi was encircled on three sides. Only the river side was open. The main force followed up under the king and encamped at a distance of about two kilometers from the advance guard.

The population of Thavoi did not appear to react in any way to the withdrawal of the Burmese. When Kaengwunmaengyi became aware of this he ordered his troops back into the city but did not engage in battle. After the siege had lasted about half a month the provisions of the besieging troops became rather scanty. The Thai army was therefore faced with the choice of either attacking the city immediately or retreating. Most of the commanders favored an immediate attack,[191] but the king nevertheless decided to withdraw. We do not know what considerations guided the king in his decision. Perhaps he realized that in the long run it would be difficult to hold Thavoi from as far as Thailand. And there was the danger that a retreat might develop into a catastrophe if the attack on the city should fail.[192]

The Burmese troops followed the withdrawing Thai forces but were unable to disturb their orderly retreat. After his return from North Thailand the Maha Uparat, upon receiving the news of the king's retreat, hastened to the frontier at Saiyok in order to be in a position to intercept a possible counterattack on the part of the Burmese.[193]

The second attack of the Thai on Thavoi, 1791–1793

The Thai expedition to Thavoi of 1787, though apparently unsuccessful, did nevertheless cause certain reactions among the Mọn. In

[188] Damrong, *Thai rop Phama*, vol. 2, p. 213; *P.P.R.I*, p. 173; Čulalongkọn, *Phraratchawitčan*, p. 229; another explanation in *P.P.*, p. 290: "evacuation because of fear and terror."

[189] References cited in footnote 188 and Narinthewi, *op. cit.*, p. 229.

[190] Where they arrived a few hours after the fight at Thọng Thung.

[191] *P.P.*, p. 292.

[192] Damrong, *Thai rop Phama*, vol. 2, p. 214.

[193] *P.P.R.I*, p. 175.

1791 declarations of loyalty were received in Bangkok from Thavoi, Mergui and other Mǫn cities.[194] Such declarations provide evidence of the greatly increased prestige of Thailand since the last wars against Burma. At the same time they indicated new internal disputes inside Burma.

Asaewunki had been nominated by Bodawpaya as governor of South Burma with his residence in Martaban.[195] Shortly afterwards, Maengčanča was appointed governor of Thavoi under Asaewunki. When Asaewunki died in 1790, Maengčanča entertained the hope of rising to the rank of governor of South Burma. Bodawpaya, however, appointed one Mangčalesu.[196] Maengčanča forthwith refused to make any deliveries to Martaban under the pretense that he could not collect anything from the impoverished population. As Maengčanča remained unresponsive even after repeated admonitions, Bodawpaya commanded Marunwǫnpo to assume the position of governor of Thavoi and to bring Maengčanča to Amarapura for judgment. Maengčanča received word of this command. He let the deputy governor of Thavoi draw himself up with 500 men at a distance of about eight kilometers from the city and had Marunwǫnpo and his followers killed upon their arrival.[197] Maengčanča then endeavored to persuade the remaining southern cities to secede from Burma and to put themselves under the control of Thailand.

On the third day of the waning moon in the fourth lunar month of 2334 (1791), a legation from Thavoi arrived in Bangkok with a letter having the following contents:[198]

> He, the governor of Thavoi, as well as his ancestors before him had long been in the service of the kings of Ava. He had never been guilty of any offense and therefore it was not right of Bodawpaya to appoint the Mangčalesu rather than himself as the governor of southern Burma. The new governor had

[194] Narinthewi, *op. cit.*, p. 229; Čulalongkǫn, *Phraratchawitčan*, p. 230; Damrong, *Thai rop Phama*, vol. 2, p. 215.

[195] Symes, *op. cit.*, vol. 1, p. 266, where the Asaewunki of Thai records is designated as Mahasisura.

[196] Damrong, *Thai rop Phama*, vol. 2, p. 216, gives the Burmese form of this name, Minhalasisu, which Symes, *op. cit.*, vol. 1, p. 266, also mentions in the same connection. Compare Phraison Salarak, *op. cit.*, p. 39.

[197] Narinthewi, *op. cit.*, p. 228; Damrong, *Thai rop Phama*, vol. 2, p. 216, with reference to the Burmese chronicle, but in the translation of Phraison Salarak this event is not mentioned; *P.P.R.I*, p. 211.

[198] *P.P.R.I*, pp. 213 *et seq.*; Narinthewi, *op. cit.*, pp. 229 *et seq.*

> demanded from 200 to 300 *chang*[199] of silver from the southern cities, and this had made the population very angry. He had killed the governor Marunwǫnpo who was in his place and, in agreement with the governor of Mergui and Tenasserim, was now addressing himself to Bangkok with the request that the southern cities should once again be considered as vassals of Thailand.

The governor requested that Thai troops be sent to Thavoi as protection against an attack on the part of Bodawpaya.[200] Then he, Maengčanča, would take Martaban, Rangoon and other cities of Burma.

Rama I received the legation in a friendly manner.[201] Gifts were exchanged. The envoy from Thavoi also handed over a letter from a female relative of the king. She had been carried off from Ayuthaya in 1767 and was living as a nun in Thavoi.[202]

Details of the immediate reaction in Bangkok to the letter of the Maengčanča are not known to us. In 1792, *i.e.*, at least eight months after the date of the arrival of the legation, a detachment of 5,000 men under the Phraya Yomarat was sent to defend Thavoi.[203] Later a further army under the Maha Uparat set off from Kančanaburi in the direction of Saiyok, where they intended to await further news of the Phraya Yomarat.

Meanwhile, the Phraya Yomarat had arrived in Thavoi. The officials of the city came to greet him and to let him know that arrangements had been made for supplies for his troops. However, the governor himself did not appear to greet him, although this was customary under such circumstances. It was not until the Phraya Yomarat had remonstrated about the matter that Maengčanča came out from the city. Thereupon the Phraya Yomarat put Thavoi under the protection of the king of Thailand and stationed a detachment of his troops in the city. The remaining troops encamped beyond the walls of Thavoi. The royal niece and other Thai who had been deported to Thavoi were

[199] One *chang* is equal to 604.53 grams.

[200] See also *Phongsawadan Mǫn Phama*, p. 382.

[201] *P.P.R.I*, p. 215.

[202] This relative was the daughter of the eldest brother of Rama I, the Phra Čau Tamarong, who in *P.P.R.I*, p. 215, and in Čulalongkǫn, *Phraratchawitčan*, pp. 230, 232, is designated as Čau Chi, but in Damrong, *Thai rop Phama*, vol. 2, p. 217, as Čau Fa Krom Khun Ramin Suda.

[203] *P.P.R.I*, p. 220; *P.P.*, p. 340.

brought to the camp of the Maha Uparat at the Mae Nam Nọi and from there were sent to Bangkok.[204]

News of the behavior of the governor of Thavoi[205] came to Bangkok, where it created suspicion. The king ordered the Maha Uparat to investigate the situation on the spot. After his arrival in Thavoi the Phraya Yomarat reported that it was not possible to trust the Maengčanča[206] whose behavior was not upright. The Phraya Yomarat suggested that Thavoi be destroyed and the population be evacuated. The Maha Uparat agreed and gave orders to this effect.[207] However, Rama I opposed such measures very strongly.[208] Nevertheless, the destruction of Thavoi and the evacuation of its population had already begun. The king had meanwhile arrived at the camp at the Mae Nam Nọi and angrily ordered that arrangements be made for the repatriation of the population to its former dwelling places.[209]

It was the intention of Rama I to carry the war farther into Burmese territory. He had the governor of Saiyok reconnoiter the exact distance between the Pass of the Three Pagodas, Martaban and Pegu.[210] But this time, too, matters did not develop to the point of a large-scale attack on Burma. From the viewpoint of the present day observer Thai strategy appears to have been vacillating and indecisive. Whatever the reasons for this may have been, the result was that the supreme military command of the Thai drifted into a dismal state characterized by strategic conceptions singularly lacking in clarity.

Meanwhile, Bodawpaya put the Munyi Mahasethawase[211] with

[204] *P.P.R.I*, p. 221.

[205] Damrong, *Thai rop Phama*, vol. 2, p. 219, believes that the behavior of the Maengčanča is to be explained by his personal disappointment at not having been appointed by Rama I as sovereign ruler (*čau prathet*) of Thavoi. In the Thai records no indications are to be found to support this idea, which, however, may be true.

[206] According to Damrong, *Thai rop Phama*, vol. 2, p. 220, the Phraya Yomarat informed the Maha Uparat that in Thavoi the situation was being examined in a critical spirit. The attitude with regard to an alliance with Thailand was negative, for it would be difficult for that country in the long run to hold Thavoi against Burmese attacks because of the facts of geography. This is true, but the statement cannot be verified in the known records.

[207] According to *P.P.R.I*, p. 221, and *P.P.*, p. 341, one may suppose that the destruction of the city had already begun at the command of the Phraya Yomarat; see also Phraison Salarak, *op. cit.*, p. 48.

[208] *P.P.R.I*, p. 224; *P.P.*, p. 344.

[209] It does appear, however, that at least a part of the Thavoi population was nevertheless evacuated to Bangkok and located in the vicinity of Wat Saket.

[210] *P.P.*, pp. 342 *et seq.*

[211] Symes, *op. cit.*, vol. 1, p. 267, mentions Sombi Minki and Attawun Mien as Burmese generals. In Phraison Salarak, *op. cit.*, p. 42, Mingyi Maha Thettawshe is mentioned as commander.

10,000 men under the following marching orders: Starting from Martaban, they were to take Thavoi once again. However, the Burmese general did not attack the Thai troops which were encamped before the city, for they appeared to be superior in numbers; instead he asked for further support from Ava.[212] Thereupon Nemayosingkhaya was sent to Martaban with reinforcements. Meanwhile, the eldest son of Bodawpaya drew up another offensive army[213] at Amarapura.

In 1793, in the sixth lunar month, the latter advanced to Rangoon. The Burmese generals, who were still waiting in a state of idleness, therefore decided to attack Thavoi and charged one Makdiyong with this task. The latter first encountered the Mọn troops under the Čau Phraya Maha Yotha, who immediately received reinforcements from Thavoi. The Burmese were defeated and fled back to Martaban, where during the ensuing rainy season they constructed fortified camps and made preparations for a new attack.

The Thai armies also prepared for further conflict. Apparently the plan to conquer the entire Mọn territory of Burma up to Martaban and Rangoon had not yet been abandoned. There were also further plans for an attack on Central Burma,[214] if circumstances should make this possible, and there were hopes that the Mọn people would actively participate in this matter.

Čau Phraya Ratanaphiphit and Čau Phraya Mahasena joined the troops of the Phraya Yomarat, which were stationed at Thavoi. The Phraya Kalahom Ratchasena was charged with the task of levying troops in Cambodia and taking them under his command; and the Phraya Kraikosa was given the same task in Laos. Rama I himself took over the command of the land armies while at the same time the Maha Uparat was to attack the cities of southern Burma with naval forces.[215] Altogether the strength of the Thai army at this time may have amounted to 40,000 men.[216]

[212] Damrong, *Thai rop Phama*, vol. 2, p. 222. This and the following occurrences are not mentioned in the Thai accounts and are reconstructed here simply on the basis of statements made by Damrong, who in turn declares that what he says is based on Burmese source material. Compare Phraison Salarak, *op. cit.*, pp. 42 *et seq.*

[213] Which, according to Damrong, *Thai rop Phama*, vol. 2, p. 229, is alleged to have amounted to 50,000 men.

[214] *P.P.R.I*, p. 227; *P.P.*, p. 347; Phraison Salarak, *op. cit.*, p. 43.

[215] This campaign of the Maha Uparat is described by him in his *Nirat (phleng yau) sadet pai ti Mŭang Phama 2336*. According to the Burmese *Hmannan Yazawindawgyi*, the Maha Uparat with 40,000 soldiers was encamped near Thavoi; see Phraison Salarak, *op. cit.*, p. 42.

[216] On this point the Thai and the Burmese records agree; see *P.P.R.I*, p. 228, and Phraison Salarak, *op. cit.*, p. 42.

The army of the Maha Uparat assembled in the seventh or eighth lunar month at Chumphọn. The Phraya Kalahom brought his troops together with those stationed at Thavoi.[217] Meanwhile the Burmese main force set out from Rangoon in the direction of Thavoi,[218] largely by ship. Part of this army, 10,000 men under Nemayokyọdin and 5,000 men under Mahachaisura, marched to Martaban in order to intercept any Thai troops which might approach from Thavoi.[219]

A Thai army grouped itself around Thavoi for its defense.[220] Phraya Ratanaphiphit was situated to the northeast of the city allegedly with 10,000 men; Phraya Mahasena to the east in a camp allegedly with 10,000 men; the troops of the Phra Siharatdecho in a camp to the north with allegedly 5,000 men; Phraya Maha Yotha and the governor of Thavoi in the west allegedly with 15,000 men; and the troops of the governors of Phetburi and Kančanaburi allegedly with 5,000 men in the northwest, where apparently the troops of the Phraya Yomarat also were.

The naval forces of the Maha Uparat hastened north on the western side of the Malayan peninsula. However, only a small unit reached the river mouth before Thavoi when the Burmese naval forces from Rangoon approached. They immediately attacked the Thai ships in the river mouth and compelled them to flee for safety.[221] The Burmese could therefore sail up the river mouth without encountering any obstacles and settle down on the island Hong to the southwest of the city. The troops of the third and fourth Burmese naval forces landed at Mọngme and encamped at Kinmaya to the northwest of Thavoi. The army under Nemayokyọdin first advanced to Kamyọ, where it was divided into two parts. One encamped under Letayasihasingkhaya at Kamọk to the north of the city.

It appears that at the sight of the Burmese armies the population of Thavoi showed signs of revolt against the Thai occupation and at-

[217] Damrong, *Thai rop Phama*, vol. 2, p. 230.

[218] Detailed description of the proceeding of the Burmese army is to be found in Phraison Salarak, *op. cit.*, pp. 42 *et seq.*

[219] Compare Phraison Salarak, *op. cit.*, pp. 44 *et seq.*

[220] Information about this army is not to be found in Thai accounts. Damrong, *Thai rop Phama*, vol. 2, p. 230, gives details with reference to the Burmese chronicle. But Burmese figures concerning the strength of the troops must be treated with some caution, as they appear to be rather high. Besides the Thai soldiers at Thavoi, allegedly 50,000, the armies of the Maha Uparat and the king are also mentioned. According to this, around 90,000 Thai troops must have been involved in the fighting. For detailed information see Phraison Salarak, *op. cit.*, p. 46.

[221] Damrong, *Thai rop Phama*, vol. 2, p. 231; Phraison Salarak, *op. cit.*, p. 47.

tempted to establish secret relations with the Burmese.[222] Upon receiving this news Rama I hurried with his main force from his camps at the Mae Nam Nǫi to Thavoi. However, the Burmese had alreaady attacked before his arrival. The troops of Letayasihasingkhaya, which were stationed in the north, crossed over to the east side of the Thavoi river where they came to the camp of the Phraya of Kančanaburi.[223] The latter was killed in battle by a cannonball. His troops then withdrew into the city. Meanwhile, the Phraya Maha Yotha and the governor of Thavoi had taken up their positions in order to stop the Burmese attack. However, they could not hold their ground and were obliged to retreat. In the same attack the Burmese also took the camp of the Siharatdecho. Although they were not as successful to the south of the city as against the camp of the Phraya Phetburi, nevertheless, using both land and naval forces, they began to encircle Thavoi and made repeated attacks. But the Burmese were not able to take the remaining Thai encampments.[224] Both sides made use of cannon.[225]

The supply situation began to be critical for the encircled Thai army. Only the southern route to the east was still open, which meant that all provisions had to be transported over the almost impassable route leading over the mountains at the frontier. In order to accomplish this, so many carriers were required that the female population of Thavoi was also put to work on it.[226] This fact was interpreted by the suspicious population of the city as indicating that the Thai wanted to give up the city and were already beginning to evacuate the population. The consequence was that the inhabitants, instigated by a Wunthok, went over to the Burmese secretly and sometimes even openly in

[222] Damrong, *Thai rop Phama*, vol. 2, p. 232, quotes the Burmese chronicle, according to which the people of Thavoi attempted to send emissaries to the Burmese with a view to making arrangements with them for the opening of the city gates. But this plot was discovered, and the emissaries were put to death by the Thai. For further details see Phraison Salarak, *op. cit.*, pp. 48 *et seq.*

[223] This information is not in the Thai accounts and is based on Damrong, *Thai rop Phama*, vol. 2, pp. 232 *et seq.* A detailed description of this battle is to be found in Phraison Salarak, *op. cit.*, p. 47.

[224] The relevant sources of information do not make it clear whether the city of Thavoi was itself firmly in the hands of Thai troops. In *P.P.R.I*, p. 230, and in *P.P.*, p. 351, it is said that the inhabitants of Thavoi from their position in the city, fired at the Thai troops in their camps. Symes, *op. cit.*, vol. 1, pp. 269 *et seq.*, expressly states that Thavoi was occupied by the Thai.

[225] Damrong, *Thai rop Phama*, vol. 2, p. 235, gives the second lunar month of 2336 as the time of these events; compare also the following section.

[226] *P.P.R.I*, p. 228; *P.P.*, p. 349. The accounts of the following events are also based on these Thai records. According to Phraison Salarak, *op. cit.*, p. 49, Rama I intended to abduct all the inhabitants of the town to Thailand.

order to fight against the Thai. The situation appears to have developed to the point of open rebellion, during the course of which the inhabitants gained control of the city from where they then fired on the Thai encampments.[227] Because of this state of affairs the Maha Uparat, who had not yet arrived with his naval forces, commanded the Phraya Saenyakǫn,[228] Phraya Kraikosa, Phichaiburin and Kaenkorop to hurry on to Thavoi in advance. However, when this advance detachment arrived before Mergui, the commanders saw that the same rebellious situation prevailed there as in Thavoi. Upon receiving news of the Burmese success the population prepared to resist and fired cannon at the Thai when they arrived.[229] There were also sieges and battles full of vicissitude before Mergui.[230]

It became very clear that the plans of the Thai could no longer be carried out. The idea that the Mǫn population would actively support the struggle against the Burmese proved to be a complete miscalculation. Rama I with the main force was still about two day's march from Thavoi when he received news of what had happened. He then gave orders for a general retreat.[231]

The Burmese pursued the Thai troops as they were withdrawing from Thavoi, constantly attacking them and inflicting heavy losses.[232] They continued the pursuit until they reached the camp of the Phraya

[227] See footnote 224. Concerning the consequences of this rebellion, said to have taken place, different statements have been made which do not agree. Damrong, *Thai rop Phama*, vol. 2, p. 235, referring to the Burmese chronicle, considers it an established fact that the inhabitants of Thavoi killed most of the Thai troops who were in the city and that attacks of the besieging Burmese troops at the same time led to a general disbandment and flight of the Thai army. Compare the account in Phraison Salarak, *op. cit.*, pp. 49 *et seq.*, with which agrees Symes, *op. cit.*, vol. 1, p. 270, according to whom the Burmese (*i.e.*, the Mǫn) in Thavoi made arrangements for a common attack together with the besieging troops. The approximately 3,000 unsuspecting Thai fighting in the city were all "cut to pieces." The Mǫn commander, who had collaborated with the Thai, managed to get away to Thailand. A similar account is given in Launay, *Histoire de la Mission de Siam 1662–1811*, vol. 2, p. 346, according to whom there was a great massacre of the Thai, in which more than a thousand were killed. February 8, 1793 is given as the date. These details are not to be found in the Thai records. *P.P.R.I*, p. 230, states only that the Thai encampments at Thavoi were fired upon from the city and that thereupon these encampments were moved farther away from the city.

[228] Časaenyakǫn, according to *P.P.R.I*, p. 229.

[229] *P.P.*, p. 350; *P.P.R.I*, p. 229.

[230] Damrong, *Thai rop Phama*, vol. 2, p. 236.

[231] Phraison Salarak, *op. cit.*, p. 49.

[232] *P.P.R.I*, p. 231.

Aphairanarit, who was leading the advance guard of the main force of the king. The troops of the Phraya Ratanaphiphit and the Phraya Yomarat, under pursuit, pressed into the camp of the Phraya Aphairanarit. The latter however refused to open the gates of the camp on the ground that if he did so the Burmese would then also be able to penetrate into the camp. The disbanded troops now streaming back therefore had to offer resistance to the Burmese on the open field. The Thai officers vainly attempted to convince the Phraya Aphairanarit that his order was not right. Apparently the ensuing battle ended with catastrophic losses for the Thai troops. Both Phraya Mahasena[233] and the Phraya Siharatdecho fell in battle. Their armies were totally destroyed. The camp of the Phraya Aphairanarit also fell into the hands of the Burmese.[234] The Thai troops were at last able to offer resistance in a narrow ravine, inflicting such heavy losses on the Burmese that they were obliged to give up the pursuit. The Phraya Aphairanarit was condemned to death by the king, while other officers who had opposed his orders were elevated in rank.

A messenger was hastily dispatched to Bangkok with a warning about the possibility of restiveness on the part of the Burmese prisoners and the Mǫn who had been evacuated thither.[235] In case of necessity all rebels were to be killed. From Bangkok a messenger was sent by way of Phetburi to Kra where the Maha Uparat was at that time. The latter, greatly alarmed by the news from Thavoi, ordered the immediate breaking off of the siege of Mergui to be followed by a retreat. Just at this time Burmese naval reinforcements arrived and vigorously attacked the Thai troops then preparing for retreat.[236] Phraya Saenyakǫn offered resistance as far as possible, but the Burmese had superior force. The Thai troops managed to escape to the harbor of Bak Čan where they went on land. All their ships and cannon were taken by the Burmese as booty. Under further pursuit the troops of the Phraya Saenyakǫn arrived at Chumphǫn and from there went to Bangkok. And so the Thai attack on South Burma came to an end without success. The

[233] According to Damrong, *Thai rop Phama*, vol. 2, p. 236, with reference to the Burmese chronicle, see Phraison Salarak, *op. cit.*, p. 50. *P.P.R.I*, p. 232, says that the Mahasena was no longer to be found and that he could not be buried.

[234] *P.P.*, p. 353.

[235] Compare footnote 209 of this chapter.

[236] *P.P.R.I*, p. 234; *P.P.*, p. 355; Damrong, *Thai rop Phama*, vol. 2, p. 230; Phraison Salarak, *op. cit.*, p. 51. Symes, *op. cit.*, vol. 1, p. 364, describes the Burmese fleet as the strongest part of Burma's armed forces.

Burmese fleet took advantage of the position it had won and in the same year apparently attacked the west coast of Thailand, in particular Thalang.[237]

Probably while the struggle for Thavoi was still going on or immediately thereafter,[238] Bodawpaya endeavored to establish diplomatic contacts with Thailand.[239] He asked the governor of Martaban, through a Mǫn named Prakot, to convey a letter to the governor of Kančanaburi[240] in which he requested that friendly relations be established between Burma and Thailand.[241] The governor of Kančanaburi transmitted this letter to Bangkok. The Thai government was immediately struck by the unusual procedure of Bodawpaya of sending a letter of this kind through the governor of Kančanaburi. Rama I sent his reply the same way—through the governor of Kančanaburi to the governor of Martaban. The contents of the reply were substantially as follows: The message, which had been brought to Thailand by nine Mǫn emissaries, had been discussed with all the ministers in Bangkok. By 2327 (1784) the Burmese, with similar intentions, had negotiated with the Thai at Angngiu in the vicinity of the Pass of the Three Pagodas,[242] but at the very same time the Burmese had captured nine Thai in the borderland and this had been followed by a military attack on Thailand

[237] According to Wichienkhiri, *Phongsawadan Songkhla I*, p. 46, and Si Wǫrawat, *op. cit.*, p. 36; but the chronology does not seem absolutely certain in relation to the rebellion of Yiring, dated 2352; see Wichienkhiri, *Phongsawadan Songkhla II*, p. 18, and *P.P.R.I*, pp. 340 *et seq.* For this attack—2336 or 2352—troops from Songkhla, Čana, Saiburi and Phathalung were ordered to Thalang, altogether around 1,100, who drove out the emaciated Burmese. After a one-year expedition the troops returned to Songkhla by way of Trang.

[238] *P.P.R.I*, p. 235, and *P.P.*, p. 356, mention the third lunar month 2336 as the date; this would be around the beginning of the rainy season, at which time there was probably no more fighting in this monsoon region. Compare footnote 225 of this chapter.

[239] Another account is given by Symes, *op. cit.*, vol. 1, pp. 272 *et seq.*, according to whom an offer to conclude a treaty was made on Thai initiative. A peace treaty was very quickly arranged, ceding to Burma the western part of the Malayan peninsula up to Tenasserim. This statement should be noted, even if it cannot be proved.

[240] In *Čerača khuam mŭang Thai Phama*, p. 8, doubts are expressed as to whether Bodawpaya really did do this, as at that time there was still war between the powers. But these doubts do not seem to be justified, as the accounts in the Thai records are too detailed and precise and contain references to the political situation of the time. The possibility cannot be excluded that the original documents may still be discovered in the archives in Bangkok.

[241] More detailed information about this is not given. In *P.P.R.I*, p. 235, in *P.P.*, p. 356, and in *Čerača khuam mŭang Thai Phama*, pp. 6 *et seq.*, the essential points of this letter can be gathered from the answer of Rama I.

[242] See p. 43.

in the following year. Moreover, many inhabitants of the country had been abducted by them. The king of Thailand agreed with the king of Burma that captured generals and officers should be well treated and cared for, as the Thai had always let it be known that this was their attitude. However, the Thai were not inclined to become involved in ruses, but were only interested in sincere offers of peace. Thailand was free of any hostility toward Burma. If the offer of friendship was sincere, it would be necessary for the two kings or their ministers to meet. It would also be necessary to bring the present war to an end. There were a number of different possibilities. The governor could put this matter before the Burmese king in the proper way; also Burmese and Thai envoys could conduct negotiations in a friendly spirit. Otherwise, attempts to establish contact would serve no useful purpose.[243]

We have no knowledge of further negotiations or accounts of this matter.

The Burmese attack on northern Thailand, 1797

The dating of this new Burmese attack is a matter concerning which Burmese and Thai records do not agree. The "Burmese Chronicle" puts this attack in the year 2340, *i.e.*, 1797,[244] but, according to Thai statements, it took place two years before in 2338, *i.e.*, 1795.[245] It appears that the date given in the Burmese *Glass Palace Chronicle* is correct, for 2340 is the date given in the poem *Phleng yau rŭang Krom Phra Ratcha Wang Bǫwǫn Mahasurasinghanat rop Phama thi mŭang Chiengmai* by Sunthǫn Phithak, who himself took part in this campaign as an officer in the service of the Maha Uparat.[246]

For the internal security of the Burmese kingdom, now as previously, it was almost a necessity to control northern Thailand. Above all, it could be a means of more easily controlling the Shan peoples,

[243] *P.P.R.I*, pp. 236 *et seq.*

[244] Phraison Salarak, *op. cit.*, p. 56.

[245] *P.P.R.I*, pp. 245 *et seq.*; *P.P.*, p. 366; but compare these records, pp. 259, 379, according to which the Burmese in the twelfth month Č.S. 1159 (1797) sent letters to Phetburi, Ratburi, Saiyok, Tak, Uthaithani, Chiengmai and Luong Phra Bang announcing that they would conquer Bangkok, in which conquest the English would come to their help with ships sailing up the Mae Nam Čau Phraya. The departure was to take place in the second month under Insaewun. This threat may refer to the attack on North Thailand which followed in 2340; as also *Phongsawadan Mǫn Phama*, p. 383, apparently following *P.P.R.I.*

[246] Damrong, *Thai rop Phama*, vol. 2, p. 238, also accepts the Burmese statements; and Sonakun, *op. cit.*, p. 30, in turn, follows his account.

frequently inclined to revolt. After the unsuccessful undertaking of 1787 the Burmese tried once again in 1797 to gain footing in Chiengmai and Lampang and again during the time of Rama I in 1802, yet neither attempt achieved success.

Nemayokyǫdinsihasura was appointed general of the Burmese forces.[247] In the twelfth lunar month (1797) he set out from Amarapura. The full strength of his army may have amounted to 50,000 men.[248] He divided it into seven detachments under Nemayokyǫkhǫng, Nemayokyǫkhǫngnaratha, Ubakǫng, Nemayokyǫdinsiha, Maengyisingkhaya and Maengyinonthokyǫdin, keeping the main force under his own command. The first four detachments advanced to Chiengmai, which at that time had already been rebuilt under Kawila. The fifth and sixth armies were to be responsible for provisions, while Nemayokyǫdinsihasura followed with the main force.

Phraya Kawila had prepared very carefully for the defense of Chiengmai. After the Burmese arrived before the city he managed to take a few prisoners from whom he was able to obtain information about the Burmese plans to conquer Chiengmai and Lampang.[249] Moreover, the Burmese believed that the English would attack the Thai sea fortifications.[250] Kawila sent news of these inquiries to the king along with a request for help.[251] The Burmese army surrounded Chiengmai with a threefold siege-belt. Nemayokyǫkhǫng took up his position with 10,000 men at Pasang, and another army of equal strength stationed itself at Lamphun in order to bar the way of any replacement army approaching from the south.

The Maha Uparat set out from Bangkok accompanied by the Phra Ratcha Wang Lang, Čau Fa Krom Luong Čakčetsada, Čau Fa Krom Luong Thepharirak and the Phraya Yomarat with an army of possibly 20,000 men.[252] And the Čau Anu, Prince of Vientiane, was ordered to

[247] Damrong, *Thai rop Phama*, vol. 2, p. 238, with reference to the Burmese chronicle, see Phraison Salarak, *op. cit.*, p. 56; but according to Prachakitčakǫračak, *op. cit.*, p. 497, Ungsaepo and Chitsingpo were the commanders. The latter is designated by *P.P.R.I*, p. 286, and by *P.P.*, p. 406, as a part-commander in 2345 (1802).

[248] According to Damrong, *Thai rop Phama*, vol. 2, p. 238, with reference to Burmese statements; compare the details in Phraison Salarak, *op. cit.*, pp. 56 *et seq.*; but according to Prachakitčakǫračak, *op. cit.*, p. 497, the Burmese army had around 90,000 men.

[249] *P.P.R.I*, p. 259; *P.P.*, p. 379.

[250] *P.P.R.I*, p. 259; *P.P.*, p. 379. No further information has been discovered concerning this idea.

[251] Prachakitčakǫračak, *op. cit.*, p. 497.

[252] Damrong, *Thai rop Phama*, vol. 2, p. 239, gives this figure, but it is not to be found in Thai records. According to Phraison Salarak, *op. cit.*, p. 57, the Thai army amounted to about 50,000 men.

draw up a contingent of approximately equal strength and to join forces with the Maha Uparat. Reconnoitering troops were posted on all possible routes by which the Burmese might approach. The alleged intention of the English to attack the sea fortifications was very much doubted in Bangkok. Nevertheless, a request was made to the king of Annam for help in the defense of Samut Prakan, the entrance gate to the Mae Nam Čau Phraya. The king of Annam immediately declared that he was willing to help and nominated the Ọng Hikan as commander of the auxiliary corps. He had 108 ships fitted out, including fifteen "large warships"[253] with 7,720 men altogether.[254] The departure was arranged for the fifth day of the crescent moon in the fifth lunar month, but before that time it became clear that the English had no intention of attacking the Thai coast. The Annamites were therefore informed that their auxiliary corps was no longer needed.

Meanwhile the Maha Uparat had advanced to Thoen. Phraya Kawila and Čau Anu had repeatedly sent news of the appearance of the Burmese at the Mae Khong, at Chiengsaen and at Chiengmai.[255] The Phraya of Nakhọn Sawann, with a detachment of 3,000 men, was commissioned to reconnoiter the situation at Lampang. When the Maha Uparat learned that the Burmese were not there but at Chiengmai, he commanded the Čau Fa Krom Luong Thepharirak and the Phraya Yomarat to remove to Lampang with 8,000 men and to hold this city under all circumstances until the main force arrived. Krom Khun Sunthọn Phubet and the Phraya Kalahom followed this advance guard with another 8,000 men in addition to 2,000 provincial troops. The Krom Phraratcha Wang Lang with other auxiliary troops was in charge of the supplies.[256]

At Lampang preparations were made for the attack on the Burmese who were at Lamphun.[257] Krom Luong Thepharirak and the Phraya Yomarat marched ahead with their troops and put up a fortified camp at Hui Mae Tha.[258] The remaining army followed from behind

[253] In *P.P.R.I*, p. 260, fifteen *rüa kulai* and seventy-eight *rüa ngaesai* are also mentioned. It is not known to the author what kind of "large warships" the king of Annam was willing to send.

[254] *P.P.R.I*, p. 260.

[255] *Ibid.*, pp. 262 *et seq.*; *P.P.*, pp. 381 *et seq.* It is, however, not absolutely certain whether these statements refer to the year 2340 (1797) despite the dating.

[256] The same account of the course of the campaign is also given by *P.P.R.I*, pp. 245 *et seq.*, and *P.P.*, p. 366, but for the year 2338 (1795). In any case, it is important to note the agreement with the other accounts that the main army advanced not over Li but over Lampang.

[257] Prachakitčakọračak, *op. cit.*, p. 498.

[258] Damrong, *Thai rop Phama*, vol. 2, p. 241.

up to Hui Mae Sai. Around 8,000 Burmese encamped in fortified positions outside Lamphun, and a further detachment was within the city. The Thai commanders decided to attack immediately. The Burmese were overwhelmed. They abandoned their camps and fled to Lamphun. The city was then encircled. The main part of the besieging troops were stationed to the north and to the west, where relief for the city might come from Pasang. After a seven-day battle Lamphun was conquered on the third day of the crescent moon in the fifth lunar month of 2341.[259] Many Burmese soldiers were killed; the rest fled into the camp at Chiengmai.

After the capture of Lamphun the provisions of the Thai army were completely used up. It was therefore necessary to wait until new supplies of slaughtered cattle and 3,000 *thang* of rice had been procured. The troops then set out in the direction of Chiengmai. The Burmese attempted to cut off the route of the army by building a dam through the old river course of the Mae Nam Phing and thereby diverting the water in another direction.[260] But this was not successful. Meanwhile, the troops of the Čau Anu had also arrived before Chiengmai so that the armed forces of Thailand now amounted to 40,000 men.

All Burmese camps were attacked at the same time on the fifteenth day of the crescent moon in the fifth lunar month. Krom Luong Thepharirak attacked from the west, Krom Khun Sunthǫn Phubet from the Mae Nam Phing, Čau Anu from the direction of Hui Mae Tha and Krom Phraratcha Wang Lang from Wang Tan. Phraya Kawila supported the attackers from within the city. The Burmese were defeated in one day. Their commander, Nemayokyǫdinsihasura, fell in battle. Ubakǫng was taken into captivity.[261] Much booty—weapons, horses and elephants—fell into the hands of the Thai. The surviving Burmese fled to Chiengsaen. Bodawpaya ordered all remaining armies and units to withdraw from Thailand without further delay.[262] The Maha Uparat returned to Bangkok with his troops.

In the years following the Phraya Kawila was constantly involved in guerrilla warfare in order to defend North Thailand, already heavily devastated, from further attacks of relatively minor units, either Burmese or independent. The country was also plagued by units from

[259] *Ibid.*, p. 242.

[260] Sunthǫn Phithak, *Phleng yau rop Phama thi Chiengmai*, p. 6.

[261] According to Sunthǫn Phithak, *op. cit.*, p. 12; but *Phongsawadan Mǫn Phama*, p. 383, says that he was able to escape, and *Khamhaikan Mahakho*, p. 28, states that Ubakǫng was killed in battle. See also Phraison Salarak, *op. cit.*, p. 58.

[262] Damrong, *Thai rop Phama*, vol. 2, p. 243; Phraison Salarak, *op. cit.*, p. 59.

the Shan states and from minor Laotian dominions,[263] though in all undertakings only a few hundred men participated. Several times during the course of these struggles the Phraya Kawila forced the populations of entire cities to resettle in Chiengmai[264] in order to bring new strength to his province which had been steadily depopulated by war. By 2344 (1801) his power and authority were sufficiently well established so that he could take the offensive to the extent of attacking the city of Sat,[265] a Shan settlement under the domination of Burma. The leader of this region, Čǫm Hong, was taken prisoner, as well as a Burmese envoy, Suringmani, who happened to be there at that time on his way back to Ava with letters from Tongking. The population of the territory around Sat, about 5,000, was evacuated. Prisoners were sent to Bangkok.[266] Kawila further reported that he had information that the Burmese once again were arming to attack Chiengmai.[267]

The last battles, 1802. The final expulsion of the Burmese from North Thailand

At the end of the year 2345 (1802) Bodawpaya again attempted through the governor of Kančanaburi to send a message to Bangkok offering to establish friendly relations.[268] Rama I seems to have reacted negatively to this offer, as far as we can gather from scanty evidence. His attitude was that Burmese offers to negotiate were insincere, for whenever such offers had been made in the past the Burmese always followed them up by attacking Thailand. He believed that it was impossible to trust the Burmese. The governor of Kančanaburi was forbidden to escort further Burmese envoys to Bangkok, on the ground that their real reason for entering the country was to spy. We may assume that when Rama I received the Burmese offer to negotiate he had already had news from the Phraya Kawila that the Burmese were preparing a new attack on Chiengmai.

The king discussed the situation with the Maha Uparat. They

[263] Prachakitčakǫračak, *op. cit.*, pp. 498 *et seq.*

[264] *Ibid.*, pp. 500 *et seq.*

[265] Damrong, *Thai rop Phama*, vol. 2, p. 245; *P.P.R.I*, p. 285, gives Sak; Mahāamatayathibǫdi, *op. cit.*, p. 79; but according to Prachakitčakǫračak, *op. cit.*, p. 501, this was 2345 (1802).

[266] *P.P.R.I*, p. 285. According to Prachakitčakǫračak, *op. cit.*, Kawila also went to Bangkok and was there elevated in rank to "royal status." See also footnote 298 of this chapter.

[267] *P.P.R.I*, p. 285.

[268] *Čerača khuam mŭang Thai Phama*, pp. 9 *et seq.*; *P.P.R.I*, p. 284; *P.P.*, p. 404.

agreed to send off two armies immediately for the defense of Chiengmai, one under the Maha Uparat together with Čau Fa Krom Luong Thepharirak, the Phraya Yomarat and Krom Khun Sunthǫn Phubet, among others,[269] and a second army under the Čau Anu of Vientiane.

This sixth large-scale attack by Bodawpaya on Thailand may have been, at least in part, provoked by the invasions of the Phraya Kawila into the Shan states.[270] This frontier territory had always been a center of unrest for the Burmese kingdom. The Shan peoples were increasingly inclined to rebellion and plundering as the sphere of Thai power and influence grew stronger and extended to the north.

No statements about the strength of the Burmese forces have come down to us, but seven armies under Insaewun, Chitchinpo, Balaiwo, Mademayokongdǫrat, Namilaeng, Tǫngphaekhamienwun and Mayǫkphaekhamienwun are mentioned.[271] All seven armies advanced to Chiengmai. The city was encircled with trenches, palisades[272] and ramparts. The siege-belt was laid out in order to destroy the possibility of escape from the city, and at the same time all communication with the outside world was cut off.

The Phraya Kawila defended the city with all possible vigor, and he inspected the ramparts daily. Meanwhile, the forthcoming arrival of the Thai replacement troops became known to the Burmese as well as to Kawila. Therefore, Insaewun had part of his troops take position at Lamphun[273] in order to intercept the Thai army on its supposed advance over Lampang. During the night Phraya Kawila managed to get one of his soldiers, Thau Mahayak, out through the gateway by the river. The soldier sneaked through the beleaguering troops[274] of the Burmese and reached Thoen, where the Maha Uparat was waiting with

[269] The departure from Bangkok took place, according to *P.P.R.I*, p. 285, in the second lunar month of the year.

[270] Damrong also indicates this possibility, *Thai rop Phama*, vol. 2, p. 245. According to Prachakitčakǫračak, *op. cit.*, p. 503, Kawila attempted with 3,000 men to take Chiengsaen but without success and in 2346 returned to Chiengmai. This statement, however, is difficult to relate to the chronology of events. Perhaps this undertaking took place before the beginning of general hostilities, more precisely before the departure of the Burmese army, in which case it must have been regarded as a provocation by Bodawpaya.

[271] *P.P.R.I*, p. 286.

[272] The exact size of these palisades is given in *ibid.*, p. 287, and in *P.P.*, p. 406: 6 meters high, including 2 meters under the earth, and it was around 25 centimeters thick.

[273] According to Damrong, *Thai rop Phama*, vol. 2, p. 237; but this statement is not to be found in other Thai accounts.

[274] And is allegedly to have left behind a letter for the Burmese in which he said that he would return by the same route, *P.P.R.I*, p. 287.

his army. He informed the Maha Uparat about the situation in Chiengmai and asked him for a message for the population of that city assuring them that reinforcements would soon arrive. The Maha Uparat gave Thau Mahayak a letter to this effect for the Phraya Kawila. Its contents stated that the city was to be held until the arrival of the two contingents of reinforcements.

At this time the Maha Uparat lay ill.[275] His condition steadily worsened, so that he was no longer able to march. He therefore ordered the Čau Fa Krom Luong Thepharirak and the Phraya Yomarat to advance immediately by way of Li with troops of the *Wang Luong*[276] and the provincial troops.[277] The troops of the *Wang Na*[278] received orders to march by way of Lampang under the command of Krom Khun Sunthǫn Phubet, the Phraya Kalahom and Phra Ǫng Čau Lamduon, one of the sons of the Maha Uparat, among others.

It appears that the army of the Thepharirak did not advance as rapidly as ordered.[279] Upon arrival in Li, Thepharirak received news that the Burmese were approaching in large numbers—reportedly from Pasang.[280] Thepharirak and the Phraya Yomarat believed that their troops were not yet adequately prepared for battle and so they again withdrew to the south of Li. However, the army seems to have advanced to Lamphun shortly afterwards, arriving there around the same time as the troops of the *Wang Na.*[281] A battle took place before the city. The Burmese troops were defeated and withdrew to Chiengmai. The acting commander-in-chief of the Burmese, Yesidǫng,[282] was taken into captivity. Both Thai armies marched on to Chiengmai where they encircled the besieging troops. The army of Čau Anu had not yet arrived.[283]

275 "In a feverish condition caused by a poison," according to *P.P.R.I,* p. 285; compare *ibid.*, p. 290.

276 The "Main Palace" of the king.

277 *Thap hua mŭang,* which are mentioned as different from the troops starting from Bangkok.

278 The "Front Palace" which was the residence of the Maha Uparat.

279 According to Damrong, *Thai rop Phama,* vol. 2, p. 248.

280 Damrong, *ibid.*, vol. 2, p. 248, thinks that the Burmese troops were actually not removed from Lamphun, so that the armies of the Thepharirak and the Phraya Yomarat had no reason to hold back. What *P.P.R.I,* p. 296, has to say about this matter is not so clear: "When Li had been reached, the Burmese may have been able to come on and the Thai troops to withdraw to the south of Li." *Item P.P.*, p. 416, but also compare *ibid.*, pp. 288, 408.

281 *P.P.R.I,* pp. 288 *et seq.; P.P.*, pp. 408 *et seq.*

282 About whom *P.P.R.I,* p. 289, says: he was a Thai who had been abducted from Ayuthaya in 1767.

283 *P.P.R.I,* pp. 290, 295.

When he heard of the illness of the Maha Uparat, who at that time was almost sixty years old, Rama I immediately sent the Krom Phraratcha Wang Lang to Thoen. The Maha Uparat gave the Krom Phraratcha Wang Lang full authority to act in his stead by turning over to him his royal sword. He instructed him to attack the Burmese troops at Chiengmai as soon as possible. The Krom Phraratcha Wang Lang then hastened to Chiengmai where he called together an assembly of all Thai officers to whom he read out his letter of appointment. At the same time he set forth the plan of attack. It was known that the fighting strength of the Burmese had diminished. The attack, to be made simultaneously from all sides, was fixed for the following morning. Severe penalties were threatened against any troops guilty of hesitation.

The attack began at dawn. The troops of the *Wang Na* attacked first, but the troops of the *Wang Luong* hesitated when they caught sight of the Burmese rifle barrels. However, To, the governor of Phichai, particularly distinguished himself at this point, and he also prevailed upon the remaining troops to attack. The enemy camps were taken. The Burmese fled and were pursued by the Phraya Kawila. Many of them were killed or made prisoners.[284] Seven days later the troops from Vientiane arrived.[285]

After victory was achieved the whole body of generals made for Thoen in order to report to the Maha Uparat. The behavior of the officers of the *Wang Luong* army was censured. As a punitive measure[286] they were ordered, together with the troops from Vientiane, to take Chiengsaen, the last remaining Burmese stronghold on Thai territory. The Maha Uparat returned to Bangkok with the officers of the *Wang Na*[287] who had covered themselves with glory. It was the last campaign of the Maha Uparat, for he died shortly afterwards.[288]

Čau Fa Krom Luong Thepharirak, Phraya Yomarat, Čau Anu and the governors of Lampang, Nan and Chiengmai returned to Chiengmai where they awaited the rainy season.[289] However, it was impossible to

[284] Sonakun, *op. cit.*, pp. 30 *et seq.*; *P.P.R.I*, p. 292; *P.P.*, p. 412.

[285] *P.P.R.I*, p. 295; *P.P.*, p. 415.

[286] See on this matter Damrong, *Tamnan wang na*, pp. 32, 36 *et seq.*, who discusses the background of the developing conflict between Rama I, the lord of the *Wang Luong*, and the Maha Uparat, the lord of the *Wang Na*. The above-mentioned punitive measure must also be seen in this relationship. A good deal of Damrong's reasoning is, however, of a purely speculative nature.

[287] At Bangkok their provocative behavior toward the officials of the *Wang Luong* soon led to serious difficulties. See Chapter I, p. 12.

[288] See p. 11, Chapter I.

[289] *P.P.R.I*, p. 309; *P.P.*, p. 429.

set out before the fourth lunar month 2347, as the troops from the north, from Vientiane, Chiengmai, Lampang and Nan[290] were not ready for battle before this time. Moreover, the rice fields of these regions had to be tilled[291] before the fighting began.

In the fifth month the troops arrived before Chiengsaen[292] and began to besiege the city, but there is no definite evidence that an attack was attempted.[293]

The rainy season began again in the seventh month. Many of the soldiers and officers of the main force, the majority of whom were from southern or central Thailand, became sick. Moreover, provisions were beginning to run short and news was received that the Burmese were approaching with large reinforcements. Čau Fa Krom Luong Thepharirak and the Phraya Yomarat believed therefore that Chiengsaen could not be taken at that time as the fighting power of the troops had already been severely weakened. However, it would have been easy enough to take Chiengsaen because provisions in the city were already depleted, and elephants and horses were being killed for food.[294] As soon as the main force of the Thai withdrew, the northern troops which had remained before Chiengsaen were able to penetrate into the city.[295] Many Burmese were killed, and the Burmese general was taken into captivity.[296] The rest fled over the Mae Khong.

Chiengsaen was destroyed. Many of the people living there, according to accounts 23,000 who had been brought there[297] by the Burmese, were evacuated in five groups as follows: one group was sent

[290] According to Suriyaphong, *Phongsawadan Nan,* p. 139, the troops of Nan, allegedly 10,000 men, set out in the fifth lunar month in the direction of Chiengsaen. Although this statement cannot be evaluated properly at the present time, the troops of Nan cannot possibly have amounted to 10,000 men.

[291] Damrong, *Thai rop Phama,* vol. 2, p. 251.

[292] Suriyaphong, *op. cit.,* p. 140, calculates that the troops under the command of the Phraya Yomarat amounted to 20,000 men.

[293] The question is answered affirmatively by *Phongsawadan Mǫn Phama,* p. 383, which says that the Phraya Yomarat attempted to storm Chiengsaen but without success; but *P.P.R.I,* p. 309, and Damrong, *Thai rop Phama,* vol. 2, p. 252, do not agree.

[294] *P.P.R.I,* p. 310; *P.P.,* p. 43.

[295] According to *P.P.R.I,* p. 310, the population of the city opened the city gates; but according to Suriyaphong, *op. cit.,* p. 140, 3,000 northern troops, including 1,000 from Nan and the same number from Chiengmai, took the initiative and broke into the city; see also Mahāamatayathibǫdi, *Phongsawadan Chiengmai,* p. 79.

[296] Named Miowun in Prachakitčakǫračak, *op. cit.,* p. 504, and in *P.P.R.I,* p. 310, Bomayunguon.

[297] "Speaking different languages and coming from different countries," *P.P.R.I,* p. 310.

partly to Saraburi and partly to Ratburi, and the four remaining groups were sent to Vientiane, Nan, Chiengmai and Lampang.

Čau Fa Krom Luong Thepharirak and the Phraya Yomarat were arrested in Bangkok by the command of Rama I because of their deficiencies as troop leaders. However, they were both set free a few days later. The Phraya Kawila, who had greatly distinguished himself under all circumstances, was promoted to the rank of Čau Phraya.[298] Other governors of northern Thailand were also elevated in rank.

After termination of that successful campaign the Shan states were devastated[299] and placed under a loose Thai authority in order to forestall the possibility of further Burmese attacks from the north.

In the dry season of 2347 (1804) part of the troops of the northern provinces[300] set out in the direction of Khoen in order to take Chiengtung and the Laotian cities located to the east of the Mae Khong. Most regions, including Yǫng,[301] Chiengtung[302] and Khoen, surrendered without fighting. Mŭang Yǫng was used as a base for subjugating all the surrounding territory.[303]

Another unit under the governor of Nan[304] marched in the direction of Mŭang Luong Phu Kha in the region of Sipsǫng Panna. Chiengrung and other cities submitted without resistance,[305] with the exception of the Burmese troops at Chiengkhaeng. The prince of Chiengkhaeng had, however, learned of the subjugation of Chiengrung.

[298] According to Damrong, *Thai rop Phama*, vol. 2, p. 253, and *P.P.R.I*, p. 296: Kawila was "Lord over fifty-seven cities in Lanna"; but according to Prachakitčakǫračak, *op. cit.*, p. 502, the elevation in rank had already occurred in 2345 (1802). Mahāamatayathibǫdi, *op. cit.*, p. 81, places it in the time of Rama II, in the fifth month of 2357, the year in which Kawila died, but Mahāamatayathibǫdi is probably in error.

[299] Harvey, *op. cit.*, p. 271, says that in 1803 the Thai laid waste to the region up to Kengtung and evacuated the entire population of this territory to Chiengmai.

[300] In *P.P.R.I*, p. 313, and in *P.P.*, p. 433, Chiengmai, Lampang, Phrae and Thoen are enumerated, but according to Prachakitčakǫračak, *op. cit.*, p. 507, only troops of Chiengmai were involved in this.

[301] Where 10,000 people are said to have been made prisoners and 1,000 rifles taken as booty, Prachakitčakǫračak, *op. cit.*, p. 508.

[302] According to Mahāamatayathibǫdi, *op. cit.*, p. 79, the prince of Chiengtung, Mahakhanan, who had been refractory in his behavior toward Burma, fled to Chiengmai in 2348.

[303] Prachakitčakǫračak, *op. cit.*, pp. 508 *et seq.*; Mahāamatayathibǫdi, *op. cit.*, p. 79.

[304] According to *P.P.R.I*, p. 313, and *P.P.*, p. 434, the governor of Nan commanded troops from Nan, Luong Phra Bang, Vientiane, Phitsanulok, Sawannkhalok, Sukhothai, Phičit and Phichai. In Suriyaphong, *op. cit.*, p. 141, it is not entirely clear in which direction this detachment marched.

[305] Mahāamatayathibǫdi, *op. cit.*, p. 79; *P.P.R.I*, p. 320.

Therefore, he had all Burmese in the city overpowered and killed and acknowledged the supreme authority of Thailand.

Altogether around forty cities and regions of different sizes, with a population between 60,000 and 70,000, were subjugated. But this whole territory was subjugated only once,[306] as it was considered too remote and too exposed to attack from Burma or China. Moreover, the population was not evacuated after the initial expulsion but was permitted to return to its former dwelling place. The entire campaign came to an end around the sixth lunar month 1805.

After this time there were no further military engagements of major importance under Rama I, but we have accounts of additional diplomatic negotiations between Thailand and Burma.

According to Burmese accounts,[307] Thai envoys are said to have come to Bodawpaya at Mengkun on the seventh day of the waning moon in the third month 1807. Thereupon Bodawpaya sent a legation to Thailand. Again he offered to establish friendly relations between the two states. Further details are not known to us.[308]

We do, however, have more detailed information concerning the diplomatic negotiations between Thailand and Burma in 1808. This material at the same time gives interesting glimpses into the internal political situation of Thailand at that time.[309]

In October or November of 1808 the governor of Martaban sent messengers with letters from the Burmese "Chancellor"[310] to the "Chancellor" of Thailand. At Kančanaburi the messengers declared that the Phra Čau Kawila, the governor of Chiengmai, had sent the Phraya Phimphisan, who accompanied the messengers, to Bodawpaya with a "letter of vassalage"[311] and gifts. He, the Phra Čau of Chiengmai, wanted to be a vassal of Burma once again.

The command then came from Bangkok to bring the Burmese

[306] According to Prachakitčakǫračak, *op. cit.*, pp. 509 *et seq.*, the subjugated princes were compelled to appear in Bangkok in order to acknowledge Bankok's supreme sovereignty.

[307] *Čerača khuam mŭang Thai Phama*, pp. 11 *et seq.*, states that the following negotiations are known only from the Burmese *Glass Palace Chronicle;* see Phraison Salarak, *op. cit.*, p. 59.

[308] The further remarks in *Čerača khuam mŭang Thai Phama*, *loc. cit.*, are purely hypothetical.

[309] The account in *ibid.*, pp. 14 *et seq.*, is based on material in Thai archives said to be in the National Library in Bangkok and of which nothing more has been published.

[310] *Senabǫdi.*

[311] *Supaksǫn.*

legation and the Phraya Phimphisan to Ratburi. There the Phraya Thainam was commissioned to investigate the matter. The result of the investigation was as follows: The Phra Čau Kawila had indeed sent Bodawpaya a "letter of vassalage"[312] which was written on a golden tablet, along with a gift of four carefully chosen elephants. Kawila offered Chiengmai and the fifty-seven northern cities under his control to Burma as vassal territory. The reasons which he gave for his offer are surprising. The Maha Uparat had died, his son had been killed[313] and his wife[314] was living in misery. The population of Chiengmai was not hostile to the Burmese. It wanted to live in peace and to engage in commerce.

In his report concerning this letter the Burmese chancellor[315] remarked that Bodawpaya did not trust Kawila, "who behaves like a jackal who devours the remains of the royal lion during his reign and gives himself airs as though he were himself the king but at the same time secretly takes a hostile attitude with a crooked tail. This tail should be cut off to make him upright."[316] The report of the chancellor continues with remarks about Buddhist shrines and with the affirmation that eternal peace should reign between the two peoples. Gifts were sent to the king of Thailand at the same time.

Further light on the reasons given by the Phra Čau Kawila for the steps he had taken is provided by statements of the Phraya Phimphisan. Under interrogation the latter declared[317] to the Burmese that Kawila believed that affairs in Thailand were no longer in proper order since the death of the Maha Uparat.[318] But the northern regions were particularly anxious to have peace and order. Phraya Phimphisan confirmed to the governor of Ratburi the contents of the letters, his previous statements and the gifts which had been brought to the Burmese.[319]

The reply of the Thai chancellor[320] to the Burmese chancellor

[312] The following six documents used in the present monograph are printed in *Čerača khuam mŭang Thai Phama*, pp. 14 *et seq.*: (1) letter of the Burmese *senabǫdi* to the Thai *senabǫdi;* (2) "letter of vassalage" of the Kawila; (3) testimony of the Phraya Phimphisan to the Burmese; (4) testimony of the same to the Thai; (5) letter of the Thai *senabǫdi* to the Burmese *senabǫdi;* (6) letter of the governor of Kančanaburi to the governor of Martaban.

[313] See p. 14.

[314] A younger sister of Kawila.

[315] *Čerača khuam mŭang Thai Phama*, pp. 15 *et seq.*

[316] *Ibid.*, p. 16.

[317] *Ibid.*, pp. 20 *et seq.*

[318] See p. 11.

[319] *Čerača khuam mŭang Thai Phama*, pp. 23 *et seq.*

[320] *Senabǫdi*, which supposedly means the Phra Khlang.

though written in a very conciliatory tone,[321] does not make any important concessions. It stated that the people, the reports and the gifts received had all been the subject of careful attention, that friendly relations now obtained between Thailand and Burma, and that hostilities had been terminated a long time ago. But the fact remained that in the past every attempt to negotiate had been followed by a Burmese attack.[322] The offer was being made to unite the two countries into one, but it was not possible to trust the Burmese. The sending of letters and envoys was said to be a mere ruse intended to cause discord. The Burmese should not imagine that people in Thailand were unaware of the true state of affairs. Thanks were expressed but at the same time the Phraya Phimphisan and those accompanying him were sent back to Chiengmai. And all gifts were returned to their owners except for the elephants, for which the approximate purchasing price was paid.

The answer of the Phraya of Kančanaburi to the governor of Martaban[323] contrasts with the above-mentioned letter by its exceptionally conciliatory tone. However, the essential idea of this letter, too, is that one cannot trust the Burmese.

When one considers the result of these negotiations, it is clear that we have in this case a masterpiece of Thai diplomacy. A secession from Thailand does, indeed, seem to have been planned by Kawila. He may perhaps have been motivated by a feeling of offended family honor resulting from the slight to his younger sister, one of the wives of the Maha Uparat, after the latter's death. On the other hand, it may be that, after the death of the Maha Uparat, Kawila really considered the situation in Thailand, particularly northern Thailand,[324] demanded this course of action. He undoubtedly did desire that this insecure area, constantly threatened on all sides and devastated by long years of war, should be allowed to develop itself in peace, and he may have believed that this could be achieved only by submitting to Burmese rule and thus averting a new war.

In the war years Kawila had always been under the command of the Maha Uparat and had developed a very definite viewpoint regarding the latter's role as military and political leader. It is also possible that Kawila, who had meanwhile become the most powerful man of north-

[321] *Čerača khuam mŭang Thai Phama,* pp. 32 *et seq.*

[322] Even after these negotiations there was a new attack during the time of Rama II, 2352 (1809).

[323] *Čerača khuam mŭang Thai Phama,* pp. 35 *et seq.*

[324] "Whose inhabitants lived as if they were between the horns of a buffalo," *ibid.,* pp. 40 *et seq.*

ern Thailand, believed that he would have more independence as a vassal of Burma. We do not have precise information on this matter; yet the fact of the attempted secession on the part of one of the most able generals of Rama I, one whom that ruler had honored more than all the other governors, is noteworthy for several reasons. It shows the great prestige of the Maha Uparat, which the king in his suspicious way had to consider, as well as the limitations of the power of the central government and the strong position of certain governors, particularly in the border provinces.

The reaction of the Thai government to the news from Burma was masterly. By pretending to have already known everything, the effect of surprise was destroyed. At the same time virtually nothing was done, probably because of a feeling of security arising from the thought that after the discovery through the Burmese, more precisely, after the delivery of the plans of the governor of Chiengmai, nothing more of a surprising nature could take place.[325]

2. The Subjugation of the Lao Kingdoms

Relations between Thailand and the Lao kingdoms had always been complex and had undergone many changes. The extent of Lao submission to Thailand at any particular time was determined, generally speaking, by both the power and authority of Bangkok and the competence of the Lao rulers. It varied between almost complete subjection and provincialism and, at times, an almost complete independence.[326]

During the time of Rama I not only the present kingdom of Laos was considered as Lao territory, but also, at least from a linguistic point of view, the greater part of what is now East Thailand, particularly the Korat plain and all of the former region of Phayap (the present provinces of Chiengmai, Chiengrai, Lampang, Nan, Phrae and Lamphun). Moreover, until the time of the French occupation the provinces Sipsǫng Čuthai and Huaphanhathanghok, which today belong to Vietnam, were Lao territory.[327] However, at the end of the eighteenth century a certain consolidation had already taken place in eastern and

[325] According to Mahāamatayathibǫdi, *op. cit.*, p. 81, Kawila died in 2357 (1814), "after having been governor of Chiengmai for twenty-eight years."

[326] See also Vella, *Siam under Rama III 1824–1851*, pp. 78 *et seq.*; Wyatt, "Siam and Laos, 1767–1827," pp. 20 *et seq.*, with further references.

[327] On this point see Damrong, *Kham nam* to vol. 9, *Prachum Phongsawadan* and Chumsai, *History of Laos*, pp. 31 *et seq.*, pp. 47 *et seq.* See also the maps in Sternstein, "An Historical Atlas of Thailand," facing p. 7, and the critique on p. 19.

northern Thailand. To be sure, evidence was not to be found in treaties but only in the conclusive behavior of the Thai kings. The regions to the west of the Mae Nam Khong were regarded as being securely integrated into Thailand, even if the internal autonomy of the local rulers and principalities still had some significance.[328] The southern Lao kingdoms of Čampasak, Atapŭ and Sawannakhet may perhaps also be counted among the areas assimilated during the time of Rama I.[329] One may say, therefore, that during the time of Rama I only the relations between Thailand and the highly important Lao kingdoms of Vientiane and Luong Phra Bang were in a state of vacillation.[330] Thailand claimed sovereignty over these also; however, within certain limits the rulers of Vientiane and Luong Phra Bang were able to decide their own policy because of the size of their territory and its difficulty of access as well as its importance as a connecting link with Tongking, Yunnan and the Shan states.[331]

At the time of the accession of Rama I to the throne, the royal residence in Vientiane was vacant. In 1778 Thailand had conquered Vientiane which was in alliance with Burma.[332] Its ruler Siribunyasan[333] fled to Annam. With the help of Annam, Siribunyasan did succeed in again subjecting Vientiane in 1780,[334] but he died in the following year, 1781.[335] His oldest son, Nanthasena, who had been residing in Bangkok since 1778, was then in 1782 proclaimed the new ruler of Vientiane[336] with the title Phra Čau Nanthasenaphongmalao.[337]

[328] Compare Wyatt, *op. cit.*, pp. 32 *et seq.*

[329] See Maha Sila Viravong, *History of Laos*, p. 108.

[330] The history of these kingdoms with all their vicissitudes is beyond the scope of the present work. Chumsai, *op. cit.;* Maha Sila Viravong, *op. cit.;* Wyatt, *op. cit.*, footnote 326; and Le Boulanger, *Histoire du Laos Français* may be consulted.

[331] Compare Wyatt, *op. cit.*, pp. 32 *et seq.*

[332] Details on this point in Wyatt, *op. cit.*, pp. 29 *et seq.*

[333] In Thai records given as Bunsan, *Phongsawadan Lan Chang*, p. 431; *P.P.R.I*, p. 47.

[334] According to Wyatt, *op. cit.*, p. 35, in 1781.

[335] Chumsai, *op. cit.*, p. 69; *Phongsawadan Lao*, p. 235. Le Boulanger, *op. cit.*, p. 156, does not agree on this; not altogether clear is *P.P.R.I*, pp. 47 *et seq.*, where the account of other matters is also rather different.

[336] Not all records agree to this date. *Phongsawadan Lao*, p. 235, gives the fourteenth day of the crescent moon in the first lunar month, which would mean that the event took place in 1781. Chumsai, *op. cit.*, p. 69, is not clear. In the account of *P.P.R.I*, p. 47, there is, at any rate, no doubt that Nanthasena was appointed by Rama I; therefore, not before 1782. Le Boulanger, *op. cit.*, p. 157, also gives 1782.

[337] *Phongsawadan Lao*, p. 236, n.b.: Phra Čau, that means *not* a title of royal rank.

In Luong Phra Bang the ruler since 1781 had been Suriyawong,[338] who attempted to form his own policy of alliances. In particular, he aimed at establishing close relations with the princes of Sipsọng Panna and married a princess from La. Suriyawong died in 1787.[339] The succession was not clear until 1791 when Anurutha, the second son of King Inthasom,[340] after a violent struggle apparently won general recognition as king.[341]

The confusion in Luong Phra Bang was considered by Nanthasena to be a favorable opportunity to stir up once again the old contest of power between Vientiane and Luong Phra Bang, a contest always welcome in Thai political circles. Using the charge that Anurutha had attempted to enter into an alliance with the Burmese directed against Thailand, Nanthasena sought to obtain permission in Bangkok to attack Luong Phra Bang.[342] The permission was granted and Nanthasena and his troops advanced up the Mae Khong against Luong Phra Bang. He laid siege to the city and for fifteen days there was violent fighting.[343] The losses on both sides were great.

As a result of treachery Nanthasena finally succeeded in taking the city. He had a letter delivered to Thaenkham, the widow of Suriyawong, who had died in 1787, saying that after the end of hostilities she would be elevated to the rank of a queen of Luong Phra Bang if she helped in the conquest of the city. Thereupon Thaenkham persuaded

[338] *Phongsawadan Luong Phra Bang,* p. 255. See Le Boulanger, *op. cit.,* p. 197, where he is designated Tiao Vong, but no references are given to support this statement. A different account is given in Chumsai, *op. cit.,* p. 60, according to which Suriyawong took over the government in 1771, but no references are given to support this statement; *ibid.,* further information about the circumstances of Suriyawong's life.

[339] According to Chumsai, *op. cit.,* p. 69, Suriyawong did not die until 1791, but I have here followed the *Phongsawadan Luong Phra Bang,* p. 255.

[340] *Phongsawadan Luong Phra Bang,* p. 256.

[341] As detailed information concerning events from 1787 to 1791 has not come down to us, the circumstances leading to Anurutha's accession to the throne cannot be reconstructed. The statement of Chumsai, *op. cit.,* p. 69, that Anurutha received the nomination from Bangkok is questionable and cannot be verified by presently known Thai and Lao records. In 1787 and the following years Anurutha involved in violent conflict with Burma. See also Maha Sila Viravong, *op. cit.,* p. 136; Wyatt, *op. cit.,* p. 36; Le Boulanger, *op. cit.,* p. 198.

[342] *P.P.R.I,* p. 209, where Anurutha is designated as Ramkhau; Wyatt, *op. cit.,* p. 36; Le Boulanger, *op. cit.,* p. 198; *Phongsawadan Lan Chang,* p. 431. According to Maha Sila Viravong, *op. cit.,* p. 110, these events took place in 1789. According to *P.P.R.I,* p. 209, Rama I appears to have been convinced of the rightness of the charges. Statements in Laotian records are, however, somewhat more reserved. Note also the observation in *P.P.R.I,* p. 210, that "the Phra Čau Ramkhau (Anurutha) was an old enemy of the Phra Čau of Luong Phra Bang."

[343] *Phongsawadan Lao,* p. 237; *P.P.R.I,* p. 210.

her trusted officers, who were defending the southeastern gate of the city, to open the gate at the time of the next hostile attack.[344] Nanthasena was informed about this. He took the city and caused a terrible bloodbath of its inhabitants.[345] The remaining part of the population was taken away. Anurutha and his entire family were imprisoned. He next was sent to Bangkok, where Rama I at first kept him in prison.[346] Later, however, he was granted an amnesty, allegedly because of an intervention on the part of the emperor of China.[347]

In 1793[348] Anurutha returned to Luong Phra Bang and began the reconstruction of the city. Phra Čau Nanthasena was commanded to bring back to Luong Phra Bang the population which had been abducted. Anurutha died at the advanced age of eighty-two after a reign of around twenty-five years.[349]

Immediately after his return, if not sooner, Anurutha accused Nanthasena, together with the Phra Bǫrǫmaratcha of Nakhǫn Phanom, of having plotted a revolt against Thailand.[350] The charge was justified, yet on the basis of the present available sources it is no longer possible to ascertain who was the initiator of the planned rebellion.[351] One does,

[344] *Phongsawadan Luong Phra Bang*, p. 256; Wyatt, *op. cit.*, p. 36; Maha Sila Viravong, *op. cit.*, p. 110; Le Boulanger, *op. cit.*, pp. 199 *et seq.*

[345] *P.P.R.I*, p. 210; Chumsai, *op. cit.*, p. 70, as also references cited in footnote 344.

[346] According to Maha Sila Viravong, *op. cit.*, p. 110, for four years.

[347] *Phongsawadan Luong Phra Bang*, pp. 257 *et seq.*; Maha Sila Viravong, *op. cit.*, p. 110; Wyatt, *op. cit.*, p. 37; Chumsai, *op. cit.*, p. 70; Le Boulanger, *op. cit.*, p. 200: the governor of Sai, who was greatly devoted to Anurutha, communicated with the prince of Chiengrung; the latter then asked the Emperor of China to do what he could for the liberation of Anurutha in Bangkok. Three Chinese emissaries—Yunnanese—then appeared in Bangkok and brought about the liberation and reappointment of Anurutha.

[348] *Phongsawadan Lao*, p. 237; Le Boulanger, *op. cit.*, p. 200; but the date of Anurutha's return may possibly be later, 1794 or 1795, or as given by Maha Sila Viravong, *op. cit.*, p. 136, 1796.

[349] In 1817 according to Maha Sila Viravong, *op. cit.*, p. 136; see also *Phongsawadan Luong Phra Bang*, p. 259.

[350] *Phongsawadan Lao*, p. 238; Chumsai, *op. cit.*, p. 70. According to *P.P.R.I*, p. 244, this charge had already been made in 1791, which agrees with *Phongsawadan Nakhǫn Phanom*, p. 239.

[351] The *Phongsawadan Nakhǫn Phanom*, p. 239, says that Phra Bǫrǫmaratcha of Nakhǫn Phanom was already in revolt against Bangkok and that by letter he requested Nanthasena to come to his support with troops from Vientiane. Allegedly Nanthasena sent this letter to Bangkok, whereupon Phra Bǫrǫmaratcha was taken prisoner and brought to Bangkok. There he was sentenced to be flogged a hundred times and sent back, but he died on the way at Thoen; however, a different account is given in *P.P.R.I*, p. 244, and *Phongsawadan Lao*, p. 238, according to which the initiative for the rebellion came from Nanthasena. Wyatt, *op. cit.*, p. 38, and Maha Sila Viravong, *op. cit.*, p. 110, are uncertain.

however, gain the impression that the Thai government was interested in getting Nanthasena away from Vientiane. It may be assumed that in the meantime the latter had become too powerful and too independent;[352] and it is undoubtedly in connection with this that one should interpret the return to Luong Phra Bang of Anurutha, whose task it would now be to alter the balance of power in Laos in his capacity of loyal vassal of Thailand.

Nanthasena was summoned to Bangkok, where some sort of legal action appears to have been taken against him.[353] Nanthasena was found guilty[354] and was removed from his position as ruler of Vientiane. Inthawong, the brother of Nanthasena, became the new king,[355] and Čau Anu, also a younger brother of Nanthasena, was appointed Maha Uparat.

Inthawong, who was a devoted ally of Thailand, repeatedly gave his support to the struggle of the Thai armies against the Burmesé, as in 1798, 1799 and 1803.[356] The Maha Uparat Anu particularly distinguished himself as general.[357] In local wars against the lesser Lao rulers[358] the power of Vientiane was further increased. The Lao population of entire provinces was evacuated and made to take up residence again in various regions of Thailand.[359]

[352] See also Wyatt, *op. cit.*, p. 37.

[353] *P.P.R.I*, p. 244; *Phongsawadan Lao*, p. 238; but further details regarding this have not come down to us.

[354] According to *P.PR.I.*, p. 244, Nanthasena was condemned to death but the sentence was not carried out: see *ibid.*, p. 251; in Narinthewi, *op. cit.*, p. 266, as also in *P.P.R.I*, p. 251, it is said that the Maha Uparat, at the time of his ordination in 2338 (1795), asked that Nanthasena and his followers be liberated. This request was, however, not granted by Rama I. From the *Phongsawadan Lao*, p. 238, it is known that the case of Nanthasena was investigated in Bangkok for two years and that the latter then died in Bangkok. To this agree Chumsai, *op. cit.*, p. 70; Maha Sila Viravong, *op. cit.*, p. 110; and Wyatt, *op. cit.*, p. 38. Le Boulanger, *op. cit.*, p. 158, is uncertain.

[355] The date of Inthawong's succession to the throne is variously given, depending on the dating of Nanthasena's recall (compare footnote 350). In *P.P.R.I*, p. 244; *P.P.*, p. 365, and in Le Boulanger, *op. cit.*, p. 158, 1792 is given; but in *Phongsawadan Lao*, p. 238; and in Chumsai, *op. cit.*, p. 70, the date is 1795. Wyatt, *op. cit.*, p. 36, gives 1791 or 1792.

[356] See pp. 84, 88.

[357] See Chumsai, *op. cit.*, p. 70; and Wyatt, *op. cit.*, p. 38.

[358] Among others against Thaeng and Phuon, 1792, *Phongsawadan Luong Phra Bang*, p. 257; Rithirǫngrǫnachet, *Phongsawadan Mŭang Thaeng*, p. 79; numerous fights against Chiengkhuong and attempted interferences in the internal affairs of Čampasak, Chumsai, *op. cit.*, p. 71, and in the internal affairs of Phanom, see *Phongsawadan Phanom*, p. 241; compare also Rithirǫngrǫnachet, *Phongsawadan Mŭang Thaeng*, pp. 79 *et seq.*, and *Phongsawadan Mŭang Lai*, pp. 31 *et seq.*

[359] See, for example, *Phongsawadan Luong Phra Bang*, p. 257: evacuation of the Lao from Thaeng and Phuong to Phetburi and Bangkok; compare also Suriyaphong, *op. cit.*, pp. 128 *et seq.*

After the death of Inthawong, Anu succeeded to the throne of Vientiane[360] as Somdet Phra Čau Anuwong.[361] Anu was one of the most capable and efficient rulers that the kingdom of Vientiane has ever had; yet during the time of Rama III he nearly brought his country to ruin by getting it entangled in extraordinarily bloody and violent struggles with the mightier Thailand, thereby provoking an appropriate retaliation against his country on the part of the Thai armies.[362] During the reign of Rama I, however, Anu received full support and recognition from the court of Bangkok.

The Thai government was repeatedly obliged to intervene in the political affairs of southern Laos. The local chronicles continually report changes of boundary, new establishments and battles for supremacy in these small, remote regions.[363] The Thai government in settling these matters was repeatedly obliged to intervene by either peaceful or military means in order to support its boundaries, to prevent any concentrations of power from assembling there, or to make sure that other powers would have no opportunity to interfere—particularly Annam with its new-found strength. From the chronicles one gets the impression that right and wrong were mostly determined in Bangkok according to the personal prestige of the Lao ruler.

In 1791 there were disorders in Čampasak. A certain Chiengkaeo, who created around himself the atmosphere of a person in possession of magical powers, joined up with a crowd of people who had come together and attacked the city of Čampasak.[364] It was known to Chiengkaeo that the king of Čampasak, Chaiyakuman, was sick. Upon receiving news of the siege of the city Chaiyakuman died in his eighty-second year. Čampasak then was taken by the mobs of Chiengkaeo. Next,

[360] The date of Inthawong's death is variously given, in *P.P.R.I*, p. 315, in *P.P.*, p. 435, in Wyatt, *op. cit.*, p. 39 and in Maha Sila Viravong, *op. cit.*, p. 111, as 2347 (1804). In *Phongsawadan Lao*, p. 238, and in Chumsai, *op. cit.*, p. 70, 1803 is given; in Le Boulanger, *op. cit.*, p. 159, 1805.

[361] Or—according to *Phongsawadan Lao*, p. 239—Somdet Phra Chaiyachetthathirat III.

[362] For this point, see in particular Vella, *Siam under Rama III 1824–1851*, pp. 80 *et seq.;* Maha Sila Viravong, *op. cit.*, pp. 111 *et seq.;* Wyatt, *op. cit.*, pp. 40 *et seq.*

[363] Amǫrawongwičit, *Phongsawadan Isan*, pp. 53 *et seq.;* Amǫrawongwičit, *Tamnan Čampasak*, pp. 35 *et seq.; Khamhaikan Mŭang Attapŭ*, p. 222; *Phongsawadan Phanom*, pp. 240 *et seq.* See also Rithirǫngrǫnachet, *Phongsawadan Mŭang Lai*, pp. 32 *et seq.*, who for the region of Lai (northern Laos) gives the average population of the *mŭang*, the provincial town, as from 100 to 300; the same estimate may be valid for southern Laos.

[364] Amǫrawongwičit, *Phongsawadan Isan*, p. 53; Amǫrawongwičit, *Tamnan Čampasak*, p. 35; Chumsai, *op. cit.*, p. 67; Maha Sila Viravong, *op. cit.*, p. 143; Wyatt, *op. cit.*, p. 34.

Rama I ordered the governor of Nakhọn Ratchasima to restore order in Čampasak and to condemn Chiengkaeo. In the meantime, however, the rulers of other principalities which lay nearby, Phra Prathumsunarat[365] and Thau Faina, had assembled troops at the village of Singtha.[366] Fighting broke out against the mobs of Chiengkaeo at Kaengtana. Chiengkaeo was taken prisoner and beheaded. Thau Faina was appointed the new ruler of Čampasak with the name Čau Phra Wichaiyarat Khatiyawongsa.[367] Khatiyawongsa then extended the boundaries of Čampasak and appointed his relatives as governors of the surrounding regions.[368] He paid tribute to Bangkok by sending along things which were obtainable in his poor land and at the same time of interest to the mighty capital city of Bangkok: honey, fragrant flower water and silk.[369]

3. The Reconquest and Extension of the Malayan Dependencies

In the general confusion and trouble after 1767 the northern Malayan sultanates, which had never fully integrated themselves into the Thai kingdom, again withdrew from the supreme control of the Thai government. In view of the differences of race and, above all, of religion, it is easy enough to understand that the Malayans did not feel themselves drawn toward Thailand. Therefore, a really effective vassalage was possible only when Thailand was strong enough to exercise effective control over the sultanates.[370] Thai pretentions to control over the regions were not based on legal title voluntarily accepted by the Malayan states but simply on the claims of the stronger to extend its boundaries at the expense of the weaker, together, perhaps, with declarations of loyalty made under compulsion at the time of earlier conquests.

After the end of the first Burmese war and the expulsion of the

[365] Chumsai, *op. cit.*, p. 67, designates him as Khamphong, Prince of Wing Donkhong.

[366] Today: Yasothọn.

[367] See Maha Sila Viravong, *op. cit.*, pp. 143 *et seq.*

[368] Detailed information in Amọrawongwičit, *Phongsawadan Isan*, p. 54.

[369] *Ibid.*, p. 54.

[370] See Vella, *Siam under Rama III 1824–1851*, p. 60, and Mills, "British Malaya," p. 38: "When the (East-India) Company occupied Penang Kedah was practically independent. Siam had been overrun by the Burmese. . . . Recovering . . . [Siam] attempted to compel the unwilling Malay states to abandon their independence and submit to its harsh and capricious overlordship"; which is, of course, the British point of view; see also p. 128.

Burmese armies from the Thai zone of the Malayan peninsula,[371] the command went out to the Maha Uparat[372] that he should again bring the Malayan sultanates[373] under the dominion of Bangkok.

The Maha Uparat and the Phraya Kalahom, Phraya Senaphuthọn, the governor of Phathalung, among others, encamped with their troops at Songkhla. From this place emissaries were sent to the sultans of Patani and Kedah (Saiburi) with the demand to recognize once again the supreme sovereignty of Thailand, and as a symbol of submission they were to send "trees of gold and silver"[374] to Bangkok.

The sultan of Patani was not willing to comply with this demand,[375] although the Maha Uparat was waiting with greatly superior forces at a distance of only a few days march and there could be no doubt about the outcome of a battle. The pride of Patani was in two cannons[376] which they were confident would provide adequate protection. Moreover, the city was well equipped with supplies and other weapons.

However, Patani was taken in the first attack without effort. There was a fight at Yiring, in which the troops of Patani were overwhelmed and fled.[377] The Phraya Kalahom asked the Palatčana of Songkhla to pursue them, as the latter had good knowledge of this territory. There was a new fight in the course of which Patani's commander, Pakalan, was killed by a bullet. Meanwhile, the Maha Uparat had appeared before Patani[378] with several ships. Many supplies and riches were taken as booty.

[371] See p. 62.

[372] According to Damrong, *Thai rop Phama,* vol. 2, p. 190; but according to *P.P.R.I*, p. 140, this was probably an independent decision on the part of the Maha Uparat.

[373] In Thai records the personal title *Phraya* is usually given as the designation of the Malayan rulers instead of *Čau Mŭang* (chief of a city or land), for example. Phraya is a higher title in Thailand, but here according to the function it is to be translated as "appointed governor"; Čau Mŭang is used only in exceptional cases; see, for example, *Phongsawadan Saiburi,* pp. 70 *et seq.*

[374] This was the usual symbol of vassalage for the kings of Thailand. Information concerning the origin of this custom has not come to light, as far as I know.

[375] Narinthewi, *op. cit.*, p. 215; Anusọnsithikham, *Phongsawadan Nakhọn Si Thammarat,* p. 111; *P.P.*, p. 270.

[376] Anusọnsithikham, *op. cit.*, p. 111; *P.P.R.I*, p. 141. According to Damrong, *Thai rop Phama,* vol. 2, p. 191, there was only one cannon—but see Wichienkhiri, *Phongsawadan Patani,* p. 5, according to whom a ship went down on the way to Bangkok with one of the cannons.

[377] Wichienkhiri, *Phongsawadan Patani,* p. 4.

[378] The accounts in Wichienkhiri, *Phongsawadan Songkhla I,* pp. 35 *et seq.*, and *Phongsawadan Songkhla II,* pp. 8 *et seq.*, give further details which probably

After the capture of Patani the sultanate of Kedah (Saiburi) immediately surrendered, and, after initial hesitation, those of Kelantan[379] and Trengganu.[380]

The Maha Uparat sent word of these events to Bangkok. Rama I then informed the Maha Uparat of the expulsion of the Burmese in the north and gave the command that all troops should be brought back to Bangkok. The families of Patani[381] which had fought against the Thai troops and the entire booty were to be transported to Bangkok by ship. The Maha Uparat was also aware of the fact that at this time there was a shortage of rice in Bangkok. He therefore had the Malayan cities searched, and all available food supplies were removed. Part of the Thai population of Songkhla, Phathalung and Čana, approximately 500 families, was settled in Patani.[382] Phra Čahana, the Palatčana of Songkhla, was appointed the new governor[383] of Patani, and, following his death shortly thereafter, he was succeeded by his brother.[384] It appears that there was further restiveness despite these precautions.[385]

belong within the framework of these events. But it is scarcely possible to put these reports into a definite chronological order.

[379] See also *Phongsawadan Kelantan*, pp. 118 *et seq.*

[380] As "submissive border states," *Phongsawadan Tranggkanu*, p. 102, and *Phongsawadan Kelantan*, pp. 118 *et seq.* Compare also Wichienkhiri, *Phongsawadan Songkhla I*, p. 37, and *II*, p. 10.

[381] *P.P.R.I*, p. 142, and *P.P.*, p. 272, designate these families as *khaek*, Indians, a fact which might permit the conclusion that there was an Indian upper class in these sultanates.

[382] Wichienkhiri, *Phongsawadan Patani*, p. 5.

[383] *Phraya*, see footnote 373 of this chapter.

[384] According to Wichienkhiri, *Phongsawadan Patani*, p. 5. But reports on the history of Patani are very confused: see footnote 385 of this chapter. According to Si Wǫrawat, *op. cit.*, pp. 32 *et seq.*, the Phraya Čana got in touch with the Burmese secretly in order to arrange a joint attack on Songkhla. The brother of Čana, who was governor of Phathalung, was commissioned by Rama I to investigate this case. The latter decreed the death penalty and himself led the punitive expedition to Patani. According to Wichienkhiri, *Phongsawadan Songkhla I*, pp. 35 *et seq.*, and *II*, pp. 8 *et seq.*, it is possible that Patani may also have participated in the revolt of the Khun Rong Ratchamontri in Songkhla, for otherwise the command of the Maha Uparat to destroy Patani totally would be unmotivated; *Phongsawadan Songkhla I*, p. 40, takes over the account according to which the "Indians" of Patani established contacts with the Burmese, but it adds that the Phraya of Phathalung was also in a state of revolt and was trying to persuade the Burmese to make an attack on Songkhla.

[385] Reports on this matter are contradictory and the exact chronology cannot be fixed. These reports can therefore only be given parenthetically. According to *P.P.R.I*, pp. 200 *et seq.*, Rama I was informed in the eleventh lunar month, 2332, by Ong Chieng Sŭ (Gia Long of Annam) that the Raja of Patani had through a monk sent him a letter saying that he, the Raja, had ever since the time of Ayuthaya cherished the desire for revenge on Thailand. He wanted to begin a war and suggested that Ong Chieng Sŭ might help him. Two firearms ornamented with

Songkhla as city and province was detached from Nakhǫn Si Thammarat and accorded a superior rank,[386] and the provinces of Patani, Čana and Thepa, among others, were put under its jurisdiction.[387] After a further elevation in rank of the city and also of the governor,[388] Kedah (Saiburi) and Trengganu also came under the control of Songkhla. This new prominence given to Songkhla appears to have been the cause of a number of minor struggles for power—some of them open, some by intrigue and plotting—among the rival southern cities. Between Nakhǫn Si Thammarat and Songkhla, the two most important southern cities, a number of conflicts arose in which

---

gold, plus a diamond ring, were sent as gifts with the letter. However, Ong Chieng Sü did not take up the matter because of the assistance which he himself had received from Bangkok. He was now sending the letter and the messenger to Bangkok. Thereupon Rama I commanded the Phraya Kalahom to crush Patani. After the fight the Raja fled, but his entire family was taken prisoner and condemned to life imprisonment. This happening may have a connection with the above-mentioned alleged conspiracy of Patani with the Burmese, but the question must remain open, as the far from clear reports of southern Thai records make it impossible to ascertain the facts. The same thing may be said of the statements of Wichienkhiri, *Phongsawadan Patani*, p. 7, according to which there were robberies on the border between Patani and Songkhla and that in the course of the conflict which had arisen Patani was divided into seven districts and put under the control of Songkhla. These seven districts were Patani, Yiring, Saiburi, Nongčik, Raman, Rangae and Yala. Another account of the year 2332 is given by Wichienkhiri, *Phongsawadan Songkhla I*, pp. 42 *et seq*., and *II*, pp. 15 *et seq*. According to this account an Indian magician, Tosayetama, incited the Phraya of Patani to attack Songkhla. Bangkok was informed of the forthcoming attack and the governor of Nakhǫn Si Thammarat was then instructed to hasten to the assistance of Songkhla. There were several battles, in the course of which the troops of Patani were defeated and the city itself was taken. According to Si Wǫrawat, *op. cit*., p. 34, Patani also took part, in 2334 (or 2336?), in the attacks of the Indian Sieya on Songkhla; see later and footnote 391 of this chapter. There is, however, no account of this in the other chronicles.

[386] As *mŭang tri*. However, there are conflicting statements about the date of this. According to *P.P.R.I*, p. 145; Wichienkhiri, *Phongsawadan Patani*, p. 5; Si Wǫrawat, *op. cit*., p. 33, it appears that this was 2328 or 2329; however, Wichienkhiri, *Phongsawadan Songkhla I*, pp. 32 *et seq*. and *II*, p. 7, places this event immediately after the succession to the throne of Rama I, therefore in 2325; so does *Prawat sankhep phra čau Nakhǫn Si Thammarat*, p. 69, and apparently also *P.P.R.I*, p. 91.

[387] Wichienkhiri, *Phongsawadan Patani*, p. 5; Wichienkhiri, *Phongsawadan Songkhla I*, p. 33 and *II*, p. 7; Si Wǫrawat, *op. cit*., p. 33.

[388] As *mŭang ek*, the Phraya of Songkhla was elevated to the rank of Čau Phraya; see Si Wǫrawat, *op. cit*., p. 33; Sommot Amǫraphan, *Tang čau phraya*, pp. 2, 25; but here, too, an exact chronology is not possible. According to Wichienkhiri, *Phongsawadan Songkhla I*, p. 45 and *II*, p. 17, this was in the year 2334, whereas *Prawat sankhep phra čau Nakhǫn Si Thammarat*, p. 69, says 2325. This elevation in rank, however, was not granted automatically to every succeeding governor.

Bangkok had to mediate.[389] Songkhla was also frequently attacked by Patani and other Malayan principalities.[390] In general, Songkhla was nevertheless able to maintain its position as the leading city of the southernmost part of Thailand during the reign of Rama I.

In 2334 (1791) "Indian troops" of the Siëya with many ships appeared before Songkhla.[391] They probably were irregular troops for plunder.[392] Songkhla ws conquered and laid waste after the population had fled. The governor Phra Si Krailat of Phathalung, whither the governor of Songkhla had fled, gave up his city in the same way and fled into the surrounding jungle, although the enemy was not yet to be seen.[393] As soon as the Phraya of Nakhọn Si Thammarat had knowledge of these events, he set out with his troops in the direction of Songkhla and drove out the invaders. The officials and civil servants of all cities involved in this matter then went to Bangkok. The Phraya Phathalung was deprived of his office and imprisoned owing to the fact that he had fled even before the arrival of the enemy. Luong Sak,[394] the son of the next to last governor of Phathalung, was appointed administrator[395] of the governor's office; and after a few years he was nominated to the rank of Phraya and governor.

During the reign of Rama I another important rebellion of Trengganu and Yiring is reported.[396] This was crushed by the southern troops under the command of the governor of Songkhla.

Thai sources, otherwise so informative, say nothing concerning the rivalry developing between Thailand and England with regard to the northern Malayan sultanates during the reign of the first sovereign of the Čakri dynasty. One is therefore probably justified in drawing the conclusion that the English expansion in Kedah beginning in 1785 was not yet considered to be a danger in Bangkok and did not call for any particular attention. Details of the English negotiations with the Sultan

[389] The most detailed accounts of this are to be found in Anusọnsithikham, *Phongsawadan Nakhọn Si Thammarat*, pp. 120 *et seq*., and in Wichienkhiri, *Phongsawadan Songkhla I*, pp. 43 *et seq*. and *II*, pp. 16 *et seq.;* compare also *P.P.R.I*, pp. 90 *et seq*.

[390] See above and footnotes 384 and 385 of this chapter.

[391] *P.P.R.I*, p. 207; *Phongsawadan Phathalung*, pp. 129 *et seq.;* see also footnote 385 of this chapter. It is not known from what place these troops came.

[392] Compare *P.P.R.I*, p. 340; *P.P.*, pp. 458 *et seq*.

[393] Si Wọrawat, *op. cit*., p. 34.

[394] But see Si Wọrawat, *op. cit*., p. 35, note 1.

[395] *Waratchakan.*

[396] According to *P.P.R.I*, p. 340; *P.P.*, p. 458, and Wichienkhiri, *Phongsawadan Songkhla II*, p. 18, this was in 2351, but according to Wichienkhiri, *Phongsawadan Songkhla I*, p. 46, probably in 2336.

of Kedah are known only from English accounts,[397] which, however, permit interesting inferences concerning relations between Thai and Malayan rulers.

At the beginning of the negotiations the sultan categorically refused to make any territorial concession to the English, as there was a strict prohibition on the part of the Thai government against admitting Europeans into the country.[398] Nevertheless, a treaty was concluded on August 27, 1785, according to which the East India Company was granted the right to have a settlement with harbor facilities on Penang.[399] Together with this concession a treaty of defense was concluded.[400] However, this treaty was very vague in its language and in reality did not put the East India Company under any obligation. In 1786 Penang was occupied.[401]

The English involvement in Kedah—at least during the time of Rama I—was of a very cautious nature. Even if, at first, the attempt was made to treat this sultanate as an independent state, the East India Company soon became aware of the fact that from the point of view of power politics Kedah was a tributary state of Thailand.[402] The company, however, did not under any conditions want to become involved in conflict with Thailand. The sultan, on the other hand, was pressing

[397] Which, on the whole, are not very informative about this first period of the English expansion. See Swettenham, *British Malaya;* Tarling, "British Policy in the Malay Peninsula and Archipelago, 1824–1871"; Graham, *Kelantan;* McNair, *Perak and the Malays;* Rentse, "History of Kelantan."

[398] Winstedt, "A History of Malaya," p. 177: ". . . The king of Siam had strictly forbidden him (the sultan) to let any Europeans settle in his kingdom." But there are no Thai records on this point, so that we do not know what source of information proves Winstedt's statement.

[399] Thirty thousand Malayan dollars were at first promised to the sultan for this settlement, but this amount was later reduced to 6,000. This yearly indemnity was at the same time to be given for the loss of the monopoly of tin, rattan and sugarcane involved in this concession: Winstedt, *op. cit.*, p. 174. See also Mills, "British Malaya," pp. 19 *et seq.;* Harrison, *South-East Asia, A Short History*, pp. 157 *et seq.*

[400] Winstedt, *op. cit.*, p. 177: ". . . The King of Kedah has reason to be afraid of such a Tyrant (as the king of Siam) and hopes to secure himself by an alliance with the Honourable Company." This is quoted from a contemporary letter, though, of course, it gives only the British point of view.

[401] Winstedt and Wilkinson, "A History of Perak," p. 59; Mills, *op. cit.*, p. 28; Harrison, *op. cit.*, p. 158.

[402] On this point see also Launay, *Histoire de la Mission de Siam*, vol. 2, pp. 311 *et seq.*, according to whom Kedah was regarded by the Jesuit mission in Bangkok as dependent on Thailand. Accordingly, with the decree of April 7, 1784, the *curacu* of Siam was extended to include Kedah. The statement "that Thai was at that time more spoken in Kedah than Malayan" must be treated with greatest skepticism. Compare in this connection footnote 37 of Chapter I. Chakrabongse, *op. cit.*, p. 109, is also doubtful.

for the conclusion of a formal and concrete treaty of defense.[403] Finally, matters were brought to the point of a military engagement in which the sultan was defeated. As a result he was obliged to accept a treaty less favorable to him.[404] In 1800 the province of Wellesley, opposite to Penang on the continental territory of Kedah, was ceded.

4. The Subjugation of Cambodia and the Extension of the Eastern Provinces of Thailand

Relations between Thailand and Cambodia during the time of Rama I were similar to those between Thailand and the Lao states. The weaker neighbor was watched and kept under control to a greater or lesser degree according to the extent of Thai power at any particular time.

After 1767 Cambodia once again almost succeeded in achieving the status of an independent state, and a number of campaigns during the time of Taksin were needed in order to subjugate the country.[405] Rama I himself fought on a number of occasions in Cambodia as commander under Taksin: in 1768, 1771 and 1781.[406]

In the first lunar month of 2324 (1781) Taksin received news that Cambodia and Annam were revolting.[407] Somdet Čau Phraya Maha Kasatsŭk, the future Rama I, was charged with the task of putting down this rebellion. Only a few months later, however, the troubles involving Taksin arose in Thonburi, whereupon Maha Kasatsŭk broke off his campaign and hastened to Thonburi.[408]

Immediately after his accession to the throne Rama I resumed the policy of his predecessor, that is to say, the policy of maintaining the status of Cambodia as a semidependent province. The realization of this policy was made easier by the fact that in the same year, 1782, the revolt of the Tay-son brothers in Cochin China took place. This meant that Thailand's rival for predominance in Cambodia was not in any position to carry out an expansive policy. On the contrary, auxiliary Cambodian troops were demanded of Nguyen Anh,[409] but to no avail.

[403] Mills, *op. cit.*, p. 39.
[404] Winstedt, *op. cit.*, p. 179.
[405] Details about this are to be found in *P.P.R.I*, pp. 31 *et seq.*, p. 43; Leclère, *Histoire du Cambodge depuis la 1er siècle de notre ère*, pp. 398 *et seq.*
[406] *P.P.R.I*, pp. 352 *et seq.; P.P.*, pp. 471 *et seq.;* Chakrabong se, *op. cit.*, pp. 72 *et seq.* See also p. 4.
[407] *P.P.*, p. 194; *P.P.R.I*, pp. 43 *et seq.;* Chakrabongse, *op. cit.*, p. 76.
[408] See p. 5.
[409] *Phongsawadan Khamen*, p. 225; *P.P.R.I*, p. 45.

In Cambodia itself conditions in 1782 were just as turbulent as one might imagine.[410] Bangkok at first had no influence on the internal conflicts of the parties fighting each other so vigorously, probably because at that time it was too much under the pressure of its own problems. In the course of the strife between factions, in which the Tay-son brothers also played a part, the king of the country, Ang Eng, who was still a child, fled to Bangkok with his immediate family. That was in 1782.[411] Ang Eng was received in Thailand and brought up in a style befitting his rank.[412] The real ruler of Cambodia, at first merely tolerated by Bangkok but later ruling at its behest, was the principal minister of the young king.

In 1783 and 1790 there was again factional strife[413] in Cambodia, but at both times it was possible to put it down.

At Bangkok Ang Eng, now exactly twenty-two year old,[414] was crowned king of Cambodia in 1794. Rama I conferred on him the title Phra Narai Ramathibiodi.[415] The vassalage of Cambodia could not have been emphasized more clearly. The Phraya Kalahom, the intimate of the king, was nominated Somdet Fa Thalaha[416] and became the first adviser of Ang. Eng.[417] Čau Phraya Aphaiphubet (Baen), who for twelve years had administered the affairs of the country, was nominated governor of the provinces of Battambang and Siem Reap,[418] both of which were on this occasion enlarged; and the position of the governor of these provinces was placed under the central administration of Bangkok. According to Thai records, Ang Eng and Thalaha "accepted

[410] Premčit, *Songkhram Thai Khamen*, pp. 183 *et seq.;* Khathathǫnthǫranin, *Phongsawadan Phratabǫng*, p. 1; *Phongsawadan Khamen yang yǫ*, p. 95; Amǫrawongwičit, *Phongsawadan Isan*, p. 52; Aymonier, *Le Cambodge*, vol. 3, pp. 791 *et seq.;* Leclère, *op. cit.*, pp. 398 *et seq.; P.P.R.I*, pp. 44 *et seq.; P.P.*, pp. 212 *et seq.;* Launay, *Histoire de la Mission de Siam 1662–1811*, vol. 2, p. 320. Here the reports of the Jesuit fathers speak of "catastrophic conditions."

[411] *Phongsawadan Khamen*, p. 227; Premčit, *op. cit.*, pp. 184 *et seq.; P.P.R.I*, p. 47; Narinthewi, *op. cit.*, p. 209; Čulalongkǫn, *Phraratchawitčan*, p. 209.

[412] See, among others, *P.P.R.I*, p. 145, where the building of a new palace for Ang Eng in Bangkok is reported.

[413] *Ibid.*, p. 64; *P.P.*, p. 212; *Phongsawadan Khamen*, p. 228; Leclère, *op. cit.*, p. 399.

[414] According to Leclère, *op. cit.*, p. 400.

[415] *Phongsawadan Khamen*, p. 231; Premčit, *op. cit.*, p. 185 *P.P.R.I*, p. 242; *P.P.*, p. 363. The corresponding Cambodian title is to be found in Leclère, *op. cit.*, p. 400.

[416] With the proper name Pok and not to be confused with other Cambodian officials of the same title.

[417] See *Phongsawadan Khamen*, p. 233.

[418] Khathathǫnthǫranin, *op. cit.*, p. 2.

this settlement with joy."[419] And so the western provinces of Cambodia were annexed to Thailand *de facto*.[420] The son of Aphaiphubet, Rotsama, was made page at the king's court in Bangkok.[421] This was probably a security measure with reference to the loyalty of Aphaiphubet.

Ang Eng was the nominal head of Cambodia for only a few years. After a reign of approximately three years he died in 1796[422] or 1797.[423] It is said that he visited Bangkok as late as 1796.[424] Ang Eng had five sons, of whom the eldest was only six years old at the time of the father's death. When Rama I received news of the death of Ang Eng, he commanded Somdet Fa Thalaha to arrange to have the corpse brought to Bangkok and also to take proper care of the minor sons of the king until such time as one of them would be able to succeed to the throne. The removal of the corpse of the dead ruler was countermanded by the followers of Rama I, believing this to be a bad omen.[425] As a matter of fact, the burial did not take place in Bangkok, for a new Burmese invasion was announced.[426] Rama I thereupon commanded Thalaha, who had already brought the corpse as far as Čamčet, to bury the dead king in Banthaiphet and then, together with 5,000 Cambodians, to hasten to the aid of the hard-pressed Thai troops. Somdet Fa Thalaha complied with these orders.[427]

Cambodian troops were also sent repeatedly to the support of Gia Long in his battles against the Tay-son brothers.[428]

For almost ten years there was an interregnum[429] in Cambodia, during which the protégé of Bangkok, Somdet Fa Thalaha, administered the country. Yet all important decisions, including even those in

[419] *P.P.R.I*, p. 243; *P.P.*, p. 364. There are differences of detail in *Phongsawadan Khamen*, p. 232, according to which Aphaiphubet was simply to administer the affairs of the above-mentioned provinces without any evidence of the central authority.

[420] As Leclère, *op. cit.*, p. 401, correctly says, and see also p. 402, regarding the disputes between Thailand and France, 1867–1907, concerning these provinces.

[421] Khathathǫnthǫranin, *op. cit.*, p. 3.

[422] *Phongsawadan Khamen*, p. 239; Leclère, *op. cit.*, p. 403.

[423] *P.P.R.I*, p. 257, and *P.P.*, p. 377.

[424] *Phongsawadan Khamen*, p. 238, but this visit is not mentioned in Thai records.

[425] *P.P.R.I*, p. 258; *P.P.*, p. 378.

[426] This probably is the Burmese invasion of Thailand in 1797, see p. 81.

[427] *P.P.R.I*, p. 289; Leclère, *op. cit.*, p. 405.

[428] *Phongsawadan Khamen*, p. 242; Premčit, *op. cit.*, p. 187; *P.P.R.I*, p. 264.

[429] According to Hall, *op. cit.*, p. 740, Ang Chan became king in 1802, but Hall does not quote the source of his statement.

the realm of domestic policy,[430] were left to the court in Bangkok. Audiences by Thalaha in Bangkok were repeatedly announced.[431] In 1802 a legation consisting of the two eldest sons of the deceased Ang Eng, Čan and Sanguon, appeared. In an audience with Rama I they accused the Cambodian Kalahom of conspiratorial activity and asked for the appointment of a new one.[432] Rama I granted this request.

In 1806 Thalaha appeared again in Bangkok together with Ang Chan (Čan) and asked to be relieved of all of his official duties. He called attention to the fact that he had administered the affairs of the country for ten years, and added that he was now too weak physically to continue in this work. He asked that Ang Chan be appointed king. Shortly afterwards Somdet Fa Thalaha died in Bangkok and was solemnly buried.[433] Ang Chan at the age of sixteen was proclaimed the new king of Cambodia and ruled the country until 1834. The two brothers of the king, Sanguon and Im, were appointed to the office of Maha Uparat. During the reign of Rama I Ang Chan appeared in Bangkok on a number of other occasions to have an audience with the king, but once in 1808 this was not permitted.[434]

430 See, for example, Khathathǫnthǫranin, *op. cit.*, pp. 3 *et seq.*

431 *Phongsawadan Khamen*, p. 242.

432 *P.P.R.I*, pp. 282 *et seq.*, p. 292; *P.P.*, pp. 402 *et seq.*, p. 413; *Phongsawadan Khamen*, p. 242; this charge appears to have come from Gia Long, who made use of the Cambodian princes for this purpose.

433 *Phongsawadan Khamen*, p. 243; Leclère, *op. cit.*, p. 406; *P.P.R.I*, p. 327; *P.P.*, p. 448.

434 *P.P.R.I*, pp. 349 *et seq.*

Chapter V

RELATIONS BETWEEN THAILAND AND VIETNAM

AFTER BURMA AND THAILAND, the Annamese kingdom was the most powerful state on the subcontinent of Southeast Asia. While it is true that no single power was able to bring the entire area under its control, a predominant Annamese influence in Cambodia or even in Laos was, nevertheless, sufficient to disturb the balance of power to an extent highly disadvantageous to Thailand in its relations with Annam. The Annamese hold on Cambodia was frequently broken not by military efforts of Thailand but simply because of internal political troubles in Annam or dangers for this land coming from China.

It was inevitable that Thailand should come into conflict with Annam when Thailand made efforts to restore its influence in Cambodia after 1767. The probably decisive engagement which had taken place during the time of Taksin was however broken off by the Thai in 1781 when the news of the rebellion in Thonburi against Taksin reached the commander of the Thai forces, Somdet Čau Phraya Maha Kasatsŭk, the future Rama I.[1] The latter immediately led his troops back to Thonburi before the real fight began.[2] However, in the same year dynastic struggles also began in Annam and Cochin China,[3] which for the time being made it impossible for Annam to undertake any invasion in the direction of Cambodia. Consequently after 1782 Thailand again became the dominant power in Cambodia.[4]

In 1783 Nguyen Anh was obliged to flee from Saigon. Early in

[1] See p. 5.

[2] *Phraratcha Phongsawadan Krung Thonburi*, pp. 203 *et seq.*

[3] See Gosselin, *L'Empire d'Annam*, pp. 99 *et seq.;* Launay, *Histoire Ancienne et Moderne de l'Annam*, pp. 183 *et seq.*, pp. 186 *et seq.;* Maybon, *Histoire Moderne du Pays d'Annam*, pp. 183 *et seq.;* Lê Thánh Khôi, *Le Viet-Nam Histoire et Civilisation*, pp. 296 *et seq.; Phongsawadan Yuon*, pp. 6 *et seq.* See also the accounts in Cadière, "Documents Relatifs à l'Époque de Gia-Long," pp. 1 *et seq.*

[4] See p. 107.

1784,[5] after an adventurous flight with a small following, he finally succeeded in reaching Bangkok by way of Čanthabun.

Thai sources in general agree with what was already known;[6] however, certain significant details differ, and there is an abundance of facts not previously published. There is, to be sure, one discrepancy difficult to overcome in the dating of the events: Thai accounts[7] agree in putting the arrival of Nguyen Anh[8] in Bangkok in the year 2325 (1782), and in this connection it is to be noted that at least two of these accounts[9] were composed by contemporaries. However, the possibility of mistakes cannot be excluded, and in the present work the dating established as certain by previous research has been followed.[10] This is primarily based on firsthand contemporary European reports.[11]

In Bangkok it was clear that Nguyen Anh, having been overthrown, was now trying to gain the favor of Rama I.[12] Here he was held in high respect, shown, for example, by the liberal material furnishings which the Thai king bestowed on him.[13]

It appears that in 1787 Nguyen Anh took part in the campaign against Thavoi.[14] However, he then received news from Saigon, and he decided to return there as soon as possible. Nguyen Anh consulted with the Annamese in Bangkok, to whom he explained the situation more or less as follows.[15] The Thai king was indeed taking very good care of them and had also undertaken measures to conquer Saigon once again for him, Nguyen Anh. However, Rama I was constantly occupied by the wars against the Burmese, so that for the time being no

[5] Maybon, *op. cit.*, p. 207; Launay, *Histoire Ancienne et Moderne de l'Annam*, p. 189; Taboulet, *La Geste Française en Indochine*, vol. 1, pp. 170 *et seq.* Chakrabongse, *op. cit.*, gives 1785, but without proof.

[6] Particularly as given in the literature mentioned in footnote 5. In particular Maybon based himself on a thorough evaluation of the Annamese records. See also Lê Thánh Khôi, *op. cit.*, p. 300.

[7] *P.P.R.I*, p. 48; *P.P.*, p. 217; Narinthewi, *op. cit.*, p. 189; *Phongsawadan Yuon*, p. 10.

[8] In the Thai records cited in footnote 7, Nguyen Anh is designated as Ong Chieng Sŭ.

[9] Narinthewi, *op. cit.*, and *Phongsawadan Yuon*. Concerning the latter reference see Wenk, "Prăchum Phongsāwadān," p. 246.

[10] Chakrabongse, *op. cit.*, p. 103, does also.

[11] See the references in Maybon, *op. cit.*, p. 207; Launay, *Histoire Ancienne et Moderne de l'Annam*, p. 189; and in Taboulet, *op. cit.*, vol. 1, pp. 170 *et seq.*

[12] *P.P.R.I*, p. 146; Ankhong, *Maitri Thai Yuon*, pp. 91 *et seq.*

[13] Launay, *Histoire Ancienne et Moderne de l'Annam*, p. 189; *P.P.R.I*, pp. 146 *et seq.*

[14] *P.P.*, p. 293; Maybon, *op. cit.*, p. 207.

[15] As reported in *P.P.R.I*, pp. 146 *et seq.*, the value of this report is that it gives roughly the Thai viewpoint regarding the situation of Nguyen Anh.

further military help from Thailand could be expected. The attempt to win back Annam and Cochin China thus had to be made without outside help. As soon as Rama I was again away from Bangkok the attempt to escape should be undertaken, as permission to leave would not be granted to them.

In accordance with this explanation Nguyen Anh made preparations for flight. He commanded two of his followers, Wan and Yi, to hold a seaworthy ship in readiness at the island of Si Chang. Under cover of night the fugitives, totalling 150,[16] sailed down the Mae Nam Čau Phraya in four barks. Nguyen Anh left a letter for Rama I in Bangkok. This nocturnal departure was discovered, however, and immediately reported to the Phra Khlang, who thereupon communicated with the king and the Maha Uparat.

In a state of great excitement the Maha Uparat immediately pursued Nguyen Anh with the king's boat. At dawn one could see the fugitives leaving the mouth of the river and sailing into the Gulf of Thailand. But suddenly there was no more wind. The Annamese boats could not advance. The rowboats of the Maha Uparat pursuing them quickly approached. Nguyen Anh had already decided to kill himself in order not to fall into the hands of his pursuers[17] when suddenly there was wind once again, so it was possible for the fugitive ships to put some distance between themselves and their pursuers.

The fugitives arrived at the island of Si Chang and from this point they sailed with larger ships to the island of Kut, which is located opposite southwestern Thailand near the Cambodian border. The island was at that time uninhabited and particularly suited to be the point of departure for the undertakings planned by Nguyen Anh, for it still belonged to Thailand and one could therefore be reasonably sure of not being exposed to hostile attacks.

The Maha Uparat was not able to pursue the Annamese ships on the open sea with only his rowboats. After his return to Bangkok, he demanded that the pursuit be continued with warships. The letter to Rama I had meanwhile been found in the former residence of Nguyen Anh in Bangkok. The substance of it was as follows:[18] Nguyen Anh

[16] As is pointed out, even those who did not want to join in the flight were compelled to do so, *P.P.R.I*, p. 148.

[17] The fears of Nguyen Anh, as described in great detail in *P.P.R.I*, p. 148, seem simply to reflect the Thai idea of the consequences of acting contrary to the royal will. In the light of previous and later events, it is unlikely that Nguyen Anh would have had anything on the part of the Thai to be seriously worried about.

[18] As reported in *ibid.*, p. 148, and in *P.P.*, pp. 294 *et seq.* It was not possible to ascertain whether the original letter of Nguyen Anh is still extant.

expressed his thanks for the asylum which had been granted him and for the very generous conditions of maintenance and support. He deeply regretted having been obliged to leave Thailand by running away but had feared that the king would not have been willing to grant him permission to return. He would always consider himself the most humble and obedient servant of Rama I. At the same time he asked for ammunition and, if possible, for troops to support him. As soon as he had reconquered his country he would consider himself a vassal of Thailand.

On the basis of this letter the king forbade the Maha Uparat to pursue Nguyen Anh any longer, for he well understood the reasons for the flight of Nguyen Anh. In particular he knew that the latter could not expect any effective help from him because of the very difficult situation in which Thailand found itself at that time owing to the Burmese wars.

At the same time the attitude of the Maha Uparat deserves attention. Possibly his attitude was based on a psychological assessment of the personality of the future ruler,[19] Nguyen Anh: after the reconquest of his country he would certainly cause difficulties for Thailand, and all the more so in view of the fact that he had spent several years in Bangkok and was therefore very well informed about matters of state and political affairs in Thailand. One should bear in mind that at Samut Prakan[20] no precautions had been taken to ward off an enemy attacking from the sea. If the pursuit was not to be continued, then at the very least fortifications should have been constructed[21] at Paklat.[22]

The situation of Nguyen Anh on Kut was at first unfavorable. Cut off from all provisions, the food supply became very scarce; consequently he and his followers were at first forced to nourish themselves from turtles and edible roots. A happy chance brought a Chinese merchant ship near the island. The ship, carrying a cargo of rice, had been driven from its course. It was at last possible to overcome the initial mistrust of the Chinese owner, who let Nguyen Anh have the rice on credit in view of the latter's plans for reconquering Saigon.[23]

As soon as it was known in Bangkok that Nguyen Anh was still at

[19] See on this point the literature given in footnote 11, containing further references.

[20] Situated at the mouth of the Mae Nam Čau Phraya.

[21] *P.P.R.I*, p. 151; *P.P.*, p. 294.

[22] Located about 15 kilometers below Bangkok on the Mae Nam Čau Phraya and previously the berth of seagoing ships.

[23] *P.P.R.I*, p. 164.

Kut, several ships were armed and sent to his support. Upon receiving this cargo Nguyen Anh departed in order to take Khamau.[24] Ang Čuon was sent to investigate the situation in the country up to Saigon. He returned with the report that a large part of the population was ready to support Nguyen Anh.[25]

After a number of battles which were at first only partially successful, Nguyen Anh was at last able to subjugate Cochin China and southern Vietnam.[26] He informed the Phra Khlang in Bangkok of these successes and asked for further support. The prince of Tongking and other former subjects of his grandfather had told him that all the Annamese were on his side. As a token of his reverence to the king of Thailand, he was now sending his first booty, a sword inlaid with gold ornaments and a golden box for betel. When victory was won he would himself come to Bangkok. After receiving this message Rama I arranged to have further shipments of cannons and ammunition sent in support of Nguyen Anh.

In the seventh lunar month 2331 (1788) a new letter from Nguyen Anh was received in Bangkok, in which he again gave a report of the military situation in Annam.[27] At the time he asked that two Annamese nobles then living at the court in Bangkok, Ang Hoi Tuang Dŭk and Ang Thong Yung Yah, be permitted to follow him, as they could be of assistance to him in the battles against the Tay-son.[28] Rama I complied with this wish, and at the same time he sent more cannons and ammunition to Nguyen Anh.

A few months later news was received in Bangkok[29] that on the sixth day of the crescent moon in the tenth lunar month Saigon had been taken.[30] In the twelfth month of the same year Nguyen Anh also sent to Bangkok, for the first time, a "gold-and-silver-tree" about 42 centimeters high, the token of vassalage. At the same time he asked for further support to the extent of thirty warships, cannons and ammunition, so that he would be in a position to pursue the fugitive troops of Chiengsam which had fled from Saigon to Basak. It would not matter if

[24] Located in southern Cochin China.

[25] *P.P.R.I*, p. 165.

[26] Maybon, *op. cit.*, pp. 289 *et seq.;* Launay, *Histoire Ancienne et Moderne de l'Annam*, p. 189; Lê Thánh Khôi, *op. cit.*, pp. 313 *et seq.* For the French influence on these campaigns see particularly Taboulet, *op. cit.*, vol. 1, pp. 180 *et seq.*

[27] *P.P.R.I*, p. 179.

[28] In Thai records called Kaisoen.

[29] *P.P.R.I*, p. 181.

[30] On September 7, 1788.

some of the ships were damaged, provided that at least five of them were in good condition. The request was also made that Aphaiphubet,[31] with 3,000 Cambodian troops, should hasten to his help by attacking Basak. The Thai government complied with all these wishes of Nguyen Anh. Chiengsam surrendered and Basak once again came under the administration of Cambodia.

Meanwhile Nguyen Anh had made himself the master of Cochin China and the greater part of Annam.[32] He continued, however, to be very obliging and considerate in his relations with Bangkok and maintained friendship by frequent messages and gifts. In 1789 he sent 200 oxcarts of rice as a gift,[33] and in the following year another "gold-and-silver-tree" and numerous other gifts. However, at the same time he sent a letter requesting shipments of rice to Saigon, for in Annam the rice fields had dried up for lack of rain. In 1791 Nguyen Anh asked to purchase 1,000 flintlock firearms and sent thirty Annamese cradles as gifts. He also stationed seventy warships in Thailand.[34] However, only 200 firearms could be delivered to him.

In 1792 Nguyen Anh[35] informed Rama I about the imminent uprising of a certain Ang Long Yuang in Tongking. Messengers of Ang Long Yuang had been arrested in Laos. It had been discovered that he was planning an attack against Vientiane, Cambodia and finally Thailand. Under these circumstances the help of Thai troops in the defeat of Tongking was greatly desired.[36] The Phra Khlang was very clever in his reply to the request of Nguyen Anh, stating that Vientiane had been attacked by Tongking troops once already but that the Vientiane troops had been successful in a battle at Phuon. There was absolutely no fear of a possible attack on Thailand. Moreover, for the time being Thailand did not have at its disposal any troops which could help in crushing this rebellion, as Maengčanča, the governor of Thavoi, was then in Bangkok and made an offer of vassalage involving the territory under his control. At the same time he proposed to fight against the Burmese in their own country.[37] Later, however, it would

[31] The governor of Battambang and Siemreap, see p. 107.

[32] See on this point the references given in footnote 26, and *P.P.R.I*, p. 202; *P.P.*, p. 322.

[33] *P.P.R.I*, p. 197.

[34] *P.P.*, p. 328.

[35] From 1792 (2335), *i.e.*, after the rule of Nguyen Anh was established, he is no longer designated in Thai records as Ong Chieng Sŭ but as *Čau Annam Kok*, "Lord of the Annamese Kingdom."

[36] *P.P.R.I*, pp. 218 *et seq.*; *P.P.*, pp. 338 *et seq.*

[37] See p. 72f.

be possible to grant additional help. Meanwhile, the king of Thailand was now sending as gifts two bales of purple silk, two bales of black silk and a bale of paper and ink.

A year later another "gold-and-silver-tree" was sent to Bangkok, however, along with a letter requesting to be excused from having any part in the campaigns against Tongking in Lao territory, in order to have the opportunity to forage there for the supplies necessary for the Annamese troops. Rama I granted this request, whereupon a legation with still more gifts arrived in Bangkok, including a "gold-and-silver-tree," a throne-ship with a dragon's head, swords and curative drugs.[38]

Under the constant attacks of Nguyen Anh the position of the Tay-son brothers became visibly weaker.[39] In 1794, Ang Gauthin, a son of Ang Long Yuang, and six followers came to Bangkok with the request that friendly relations be established between Thailand and Tongking. It was said that Rama I was not correctly informed about the real situation in Annam, that Nguyen Anh was steadily attacking Tongking unjustly, and that in doing this he frequently encroached upon Thai territory. The sending of Thai troops was requested.

In a long letter of reply[40] the government in Bangkok set forth its attitude with regard to the proposal of the Tay-son. The government had no prejudice against anyone, neither against great nor small powers, but, on the contrary, wished everyone well. The letter then discussed relations between Thailand and Nguyen Anh and the rights of the latter in Annam in very carefully considered and rather courtly language. It is to be remarked that the diplomacy of Thailand was always characterized by the greatest caution and circumspection. Thailand's "love of justice" and her policy of nonintervention are expressed in rather evasive language. The remark about violations of the Thai borders is dismissed by saying that the boundaries were determined long ago. Shortly afterwards emissaries of Nguyen Anh appeared in Bangkok and asked to have a copy of the correspondence with the Tay-son brothers.

In 1795, 1797 and 1801 Nguyen Anh again sent "gold-and-silver-trees" to Bangkok with other gifts at the same time, including two golden teacups, firearms, swords, sugar and silk.[41] Among the

[38] *P.P.R.I*, pp. 234 *et seq.; P.P.*, pp. 360 *et seq.*
[39] Detailed information is in the literature cited in footnote 26.
[40] *P.P.R.I*, pp. 239 *et seq.; P.P.*, pp. 360 *et seq.*
[41] *P.P.R.I*, pp. 252, 261, 276; *P.P.*, pp. 372, 380, 396.

presents of Rama I given in return were powder, silk and ships. The gifts of Nguyen Anh were usually accompanied by requests for specified kinds of help; such was the case in 1799 when he asked for cannonballs and powder, and also support for Laotian and Cambodian troops in the battle of Ngaean.[42] A contingent of 5,000 troops was then dispatched,[43] together with 500 *hap*[44] of powder. However, the Cambodian troops appear to have conspired with the Tay-son,[45] so that Nguyen Anh had no effective help from them.

In 1802 Nguyen Anh reported that he had conquered Hue and that the whole of Tongking was under his control.[46] He had himself proclaimed Emperor of Annam with the title Gia Long.[47] Henceforth he would send no more "gold-and-silver-trees" to Bangkok. Gia Long thereby put himself on the same level with the king of Thailand. He did, to be sure, continue an obvious effort to maintain friendly relations with the court in Bangkok; however, in the following years it already became clear that Annam, conscious of its new power, would come into conflict with Thailand. Only a few years after the death of Rama I the armies of Gia Long were already engaged in battle against Rama II.

In 1803, the year following the proclamation of Nguyen Anh as emperor, an Annamese legation was sent from Hue to Bangkok to present another detailed report about the conquest of Tongking, and Hue and the proclamation of the emperor.[48] In the presence of the insignia of the sovereign the adversaries of Gia Long had been beheaded, and others who had distinguished themselves during the reconquest of the country had been rewarded according to their merit. Gia Long wanted to express his thanks to Rama I and the Maha Uparat, who had furnished him with weapons of all kinds, with ammunition, powder and food supplies. Gia Long, as a token of his gratitude, therefore sent him the following presents: ten pieces[49] of gold, one hundred pieces of silver, one great sword, six *hap*[50] of honey, sixty *hap* of granulated sugar and 250 bales of Annamese silk for the king; and for the Maha Uparat five pieces of gold, fifty pieces of silver, four *hap*

[42] In Laotian language: La Nam.
[43] See p. 108.
[44] *hap:* equal to about 60 kilograms.
[45] See p. 107.
[46] *P.P.R.I*, p. 284; see futhermore the literature quoted in footnote 26 of this chapter.
[47] In Thai language: Yu Long.
[48] *P.P.R.I*, pp. 293 *et seq.*; *P.P.*, pp. 413 *et seq.*
[49] *Thaeng*, the weight of which could not be ascertained.
[50] See footnote 44 of this chapter.

of honey, forty *hap* of sugar, and 150 bales of silk. In the eleventh month of the same year the Phra Phetchapani Si Sunthọn with three followers came to the court in Hue, having been commanded by the Thai king to deliver the following gifts: a crown, much jewelry and clothing, cloth, brocades and ceremonial objects. In the audience for the envoys Gia Long expressed his thanks, particularly for the height of the crown.[51]

Until the death of Rama I envoys were sent to Bangkok and to Hue a few times; they carried with them letters of the kings, which were sometimes political and sometimes personal in content,[52] in addition to the presents. Furthermore, Gia Long was careful to express his sympathy to the court in Bangkok whenever the death of a member of the royal family occurred.[53] He also urged Rama I to appoint a new Maha Uparat promptly after the death of the former one and finally informed the king in 1807 that he was deeply gratified by the nomination of the new Maha Uparat.

As further gifts for the king Gia Long sent 600 pieces of silk and 100 pieces of other cloth, and to the new Maha Uparat, the future Rama II and his future opponent, 250 pieces of silk and 100 pieces of other cloth. Rama I expressed his thanks for the good wishes and for the presents and declared that no discord should ever arise between them.[54]

[51] *P.P.R.I*, p. 298; *P.P.*, p. 418.

[52] *P.P.R.I*, pp. 324 *et seq.*, pp. 322 *et seq.*; *P.P.*, pp. 444 *et seq.*, pp. 442 *et seq.*; see also Ankhong, *Maitri Thai Yuon*, pp. 94 *et seq.*

[53] See p. 11.

[54] *P.P.R.I*, pp. 337 *et seq.*; *P.P.*, pp. 455 *et seq.*

Chapter VI

RELATIONS OF THAILAND WITH THE EUROPEAN POWERS

THE TIME OF RAMA I is characterized by an almost complete standstill in the relations of Thailand with the European powers.[1] The explanation for this is easy enough to find. The traditional European colonial powers, some of whom had maintained economic and political relations with Thailand for more than 200 years, had to fight for their existence during the Napoleonic disorders in Europe, or they were utterly deprived, for the time being, of their usual economic and military power. On the other hand, Thailand also, because of the almost continuous warfare with Burma, had to struggle to maintain its stability and to consolidate its position both internally and externally. For forty years, therefore, the foreign relations of Thailand, other than those in Southeast Asia,[2] were almost entirely limited to occasional transactions with China. These were largely of an economic rather than a diplomatic nature.

Nevertheless, according to Portuguese sources,[3] Father Francisco das Chargas arrived in Bangkok in 1782 and delivered to Rama I a letter[4] from the governor of Goa. In November, 1786, a Portuguese sloop turned up in Bangkok with a message which was probably from the governor of Macao but which may also have come from Goa or Lisbon.[5] Thai sources do not give information about the contents of this message;[6] however, we have still the reply of Rama I,[7] from which

[1] See Damrong, *Farang khau ma mŭang Thai*, p. 12; Damrong, *Athibai rŭang ratchathut Thai pai Yurop*, p. 23; Ankhong, *Ratchathut Thai*, p. 17.

[2] The activities of the French and Portuguese missions cannot be classified under this heading as they did not involve any diplomatic relations between states. With regard to the Catholic missionary activity see Launay, *Histoire de la Mission de Siam 1662–1811*, vol. 2, pp. 307 *et seq.* Concerning the rivalry between the two missions see *ibid.*, pp. 313 *et seq.*, pp. 340 *et seq.*

[3] Moura, "Relaçoes dos Portugueses com o Sião," pp. 55, 68.

[4] The content of which is not given in *loc. cit.*, footnote 3.

[5] In *Thut farang samai ratanakosin*, p. 2, the question is left open.

[6] In Moura, *op. cit.*, there is no mention of this message.

[7] *Čotmaihet koloniel institute*, pp. 8 *et seq.*

we can gather the tenor of the Portuguese message with reasonable certainty.

The letter of Rama I is dated December 28, 1786, and is addressed to the queen of Portugal. At the beginning of his reply the king confirms the receipt of the letter from Portugal and then continues:

> I thank Your Majesty for the help offered to me against my enemy, the Burmese, who are still fighting against my armies and over whom I am victorious. Once again I express my thanks for the generous offer of Your Majesty. I shall be eternally grateful for this proof of Your friendship.
>
> Recently in a great battle I defeated six Burmese armies which had penetrated into my country and thereby gained a great deal of booty, weapons, horses and elephants. . . . With regard to Your offer of help, I have difficulties in the transportation of the troops and ammunition which I need. I am deeply grateful for Your Majesty's offer . . . and would feel very much obliged to receive 3,000 muskets which, in accordance with my wishes, the governor of Goa could send to me during this year. I will make payment upon receiving Your Majesty's instructions about this.
>
> I am delighted with Your request to establish a factory in my country for the convenience of Your Majesty's Christian subjects. Your representative may search for a suitable location for it, and also for a church; moreover, priests may be sent. . . .
>
> The king of Cochin China asks for my help in the re-establishment of his kingdom. If I were not at this moment fighting against the Burmese, I would send off an army to him. . . .
>
> I congratulate Your Majesty on the friendship with Spain. . . .

We do not know whether the desired results were obtained from these negotiations. According to Thai statements the Portuguese legation was received by the king with all honors on the sixth day of the waning moon in the twelfth lunar month, and it remained in Bangkok until the second month of the following year.[8]

In this connection it is interesting to consider what language was

[8] *Thut farang samai ratanakosin*, p. 2.

used during the negotiations. According to Damrong,[9] nobody spoke English in Bangkok during the time of Rama I and his successor, and Malayan was the language used in dealing with the English.[10] The same thing is probably true of the negotiations with the Portuguese, which means that four persons were sometimes present to help communication.

On February 10, 1811, a Portuguese vessel again turned up in Bangkok under the command of Francisco Pedro de Lemos. He delivered a message from the Privy Council in Lisbon in which the latter reported to the king of Thailand that the regent of Portugal resided now in Rio de Janeiro.[11]

From the time of Rama I, so lacking in diplomatic incidents, the following report concerning one rather curious matter has come down to us.[12]

In 1788 a French ship arrived in Bangkok, the owners of which, two brothers, were apparently sailing around the world as adventure-seeking boxers. They asked the Phra Khlang to be allowed to box in Bangkok with the Thai. This request was conveyed to the king, who discussed it with his ministers. The king consented, on the advice of the Maha Uparat, as it was thought that otherwise one would be exposed to the charge of cowardice. Fifty *chang*[13] of silver were set aside as the prize for the winner. The Maha Uparat personally supervised the erection of a suitable arena and prepared the Thai boxer in the *Wang Na*. On the day of the combat he ordered the Thai boxer to grease himself. The king, the Maha Uparat and many people from the court were present as spectators. Mŭn Phlau, the Thai boxer, constantly backed away from the younger of the French brothers, who could not get hold of him as he constantly slipped because of the grease on the Thai boxer's body. As the elder of the two brothers hastened to help his younger brother by taking hold of the Thai, the Maha Uparat also sprang into the fight and knocked the elder brother down. This was the sign for a general tumult. All the umpires ran to the help of the Thai, and the French were badly treated. Rama I arranged to have the foreigners treated by a physician, and soon afterwards they sailed away.

[9] *Tamnan kan thi Thai rien phasa angkrit*, p. 104.

[10] This was also the case in the negotiations with John Crawford, 1821; see *ibid.*, note 9.

[11] Moura, *op. cit.*, vol. 7, pp. 55, 69.

[12] *P.P.R.I*, pp. 176 *et seq.*; *P.P.*, pp. 298 *et seq.*

[13] One *chang* is equal to 604.53 grams.

Chapter VII

CONCLUSION

THE HISTORY OF THAILAND during the time of Rama I is the history of a total restoration. The destruction of Ayuthaya in 1767, seen in the perspectives of the whole political and cultural development of the country, was only an interim period of short duration. Even if it were considered separately, it brought with it events of serious consequences; for example, the destruction of many irreplaceable cultural monuments. The temporary destruction of the realm was an event which had come from outside, a catastrophe, to be sure, but, even so, it was not a catastrophe involving the end of a period in Thai history. Almost without any clear line of separation or transition the new period in Thai history began (called "the Bangkok period"). In reality the only new elements at the beginning of this period were the dynasty and construction of the capital city, in which particular care was taken to copy the palace and temples of Ayuthaya.

The restoration of internal political life, as well as the regaining of the old boundaries, did not involve any changes in the conditions and foreign-policy objectives taken over from the Ayuthaya epoch. During the time of Rama I there are not even any additions or modifications to be noted which go beyond the framework of mere restoration. This restoration, however, must not be considered as reactionary, for there were no new elements present which could have been repressed. The so-called "new Siam" did not begin during the epoch of Rama I[1] but in a very hesitant way under Mongkut, Rama IV, perhaps the greatest ruler of the Čakri dynasty.

During the period of more than twenty-seven years of his

[1] The statement of Robert-Martignan, *La Monarchie Absolue Siamoise de 1350 à 1926*, p. 182, that the "new Siam" dates from the beginning of the Čakri dynasty is simply of a declamatory nature with no evidence to support it.

reign—after the period of political weakness of the last Ayuthaya kings and after the catastrophe of 1767—Rama I was able to lead Thailand to a new strength and power and to put it once again in the same rank with its mighty and generally hostile neighbors, Burma and Vietnam. Rama I must be ranked among the most outstanding rulers of Thailand. The tasks arising from the situation which confronted him in his country, above all those of military and internal political consolidation, required the ability to make rapid decisions, insight into strategy, a carefully calculated estimate of possibilities, and, last but not least, a wise choice of military and civilian advisers. With his extraordinarily successful policies, except for the unsuccessful attacks on Thavoi, the first ruler of the new dynasty conclusively demonstrated his right to the rank of king which he had had since 1782.

Just as the dominating role of the king in the political life of his autocratically governed country can be established beyond dispute, so, on the other hand, information about the general social life of the country is lacking. For the chroniclers of the time of Rama I the maxim that the king is the state was accepted without reservation. His person, the court and Buddhism dominate their thinking utterly without the slightest suggestion of doubt, hesitation or questioning; they alone were the component elements of the state. One would like to know a great deal more; for example, one would be glad to have some information about the economic, legal and social conditions of the population, but the chroniclers show no interest in such matters.[2] Instead, the royal and Buddhist ceremonies are described in every detail.

After the sixth and last Burmese war under Rama I (1802), the western boundary of Thailand was finally determined[3] and was not moved over to the Shan territory because of the British annexations until 1889. On the other hand, the pacification of Cambodia and Laos, which was at first achieved, did not prove to be a permanent matter. Both regions continued to be constant sources of unrest until the final enforced withdrawal of Thailand.

In the realm of internal affairs the forms of government and administration taken over almost without change by the first Čakri from the Ayuthaya epoch proved to be flexible enough to permit a gradual approach to Western forms of organization under his succes-

[2] Compare Coedès, *Les peuples de la péninsule indochinoise Histoire, Civilisations*, p. 2, last paragraph.

[3] But not as indicated on map 5 in Sternstein, *op. cit.*, facing p. 7. See the critics on the map, *ibid.*, p. 19.

sors without causing any serious break in the continuity of the state. However, in the realm of internal affairs the most significant act of the king was undoubtedly the new codification of the old Ayuthaya laws. He thereby showed himself to be a statesman of the first rank and bequeathed to future scholars a book of inestimable value.

BIBLIOGRAPHY

I. *Thai sources of information.* In the column to the left, books and articles are enumerated in an abbreviated form as cited in this work, whereas the titles in Thai are given *in extenso.*

Amǫrawongwičit. *Phongsąwadan Isan*

อมรวงษวิจิตร หม่อม

พงศาวดาร เมืองมณฑลอีสาน

ประชุมพงศาวดาร ๕ หน้า ๒๙ - ๒๒๒

———. *Tamnan Čampasak*

อมรวงษวิจิตร หม่อม

ตำนานเมืองนครจำปาศักดิ์

ประชุมพงศาวดาร ๗๐ หน้า ๒๔ - ๕๖

Ankhong. *Maitri Thai Yuon*

อั้งคง สงวน

สัมพันธไมตรีไทยกับญวน in

สิ่งแรกในเมืองไทย พศ ๒๕๐๒ หน้า ๙๐ - ๑๑๗

———. *Ratchathut Thai*

อั้งคง สงวน

ราชทูตไทยไปยุโรบ in

สิ่งแรกในเมืองไทย พศ ๒๕๐๒ หน้า ๑ - ๒๙

———. *Thong chat*

อ้งคง สงวน

ธงชาติ สิ่งแรกในเมืองไทย พศ ๒๕๐๒ หน้า ๓๔๙ - ๓๖๖

Anusǫnsithikham. *Phongsawadan Nakhǫn Si Thammarat*

อนุสรสิทธิกรรม หลวง

พงศาวดารนครศรีธรรมราช

ประชุมพงศาวดาร ๕๓ หน้า ๑๐๒ - ๑๒๗

Čulalongkǫn. *Phraratcha damrat kaekhai kan pokkhrǫng*

จุลจอมเกล้าเจ้าอยู่หัว พระบาทสมเดจ

พระราชดำรัสทรงแถลงพระบรมราชาธิบาย

แก้ไขการปกครองแผ่นดิน พศ ๒๔๗๐

———. *Phraratchawitčan*

จุลจอมเกล้าเจ้าอยู่หัว พระบาทสมเดจ

พระราชวิจารณ์ ตอน พศ ๒๓๑๐ - ๒๓๖๓ in

กรมหลวงนรินเทวี จดหมายเหตุความทรงจำ

———. *Thamaniem ratchatrakun nai krung sayam*

จุลจอมเกล้าเจ้าอยู่หัว พระบาทสมเดจ

ธรรมเนียมราชตระกูลในกรุงสยาม พศ ๒๕๐๑

Čerača khuam mŭang Thai Phama

จดหมายเหตุเรื่องเจรจาความเมืองในระหว่าง

ไทยกับพม่า ประชุมพงศาวดาร ๒๑

Čotmaihet colonial institute

จดหมายเหตุคัดมาจากรอเยอลกอโลเนียล

อินสติติว กรุงลอนดอน พศ ๒๔๗๖

Čotmaihet hon

จดหมายเหตุโหร

ประชุมพงศาวดาร ๘ หน้า ๑ - ๒๕

Damrong. *Athibai rüang ratchathut Thai pai yurop*
ดำรงราชานุภาพ กรมพระ
อธิบายเรื่องราชทูตไทยไปยุโรปแต่โบราณมา
ประชุมพงศาวดาร ๒๙ หน้า ๑ - ๓๖
———. *Farang khau ma müang Thai*
ดำรงราชานุภาพ กรมพระ
ฝรั่งเข้ามาเมืองไทย พศ ๒๕๐๓
———. *Kham nam* to vol. 9 *Prachum Phongsawadan*
ดำรงราชานุภาพ กรมพระ
คำนำ ประชุมพงศาวดาร ๙
———. *Laksana kan pokkhrǫng prathet sayam tae boran*
ดำรงราชานุภาพ กรมพระ
ลักษณะการปกครองประเทศไทยแต่โบราณ พศ ๒๔๗๑
———. *Laksana süksa*
ดำรงราชานุภาพ กรมพระ
ลักษณะการศึกษาของเจ้านายแต่โบราณ in
ประชุมพระนิพนธ์เบ็ดเตล็ด พศ ๒๕๐๔ หน้า ๑๑๗ - ๑๒๐
———. *Munlahet haeng kan sang wat nai prathet Thai*
ดำรงราชานุภาพ กรมพระ
มูลเหตุแห่งการสร้างวัดในประเทศไทย พศ ๒๕๐๓
———. *Pathakathawithayu kračai sieng*
ดำรงราชานุภาพ กรมพระ
ปาฐกถาวิทยุกระจายเสียงว่าด้วยพระราชมรดก
ของพระบาทสมเด็จพระพุทธยอดฟ้าจุฬาโลก in
ประชุมพระนิพนธ์เบ็ดเตล็ด พศ ๒๕๐๔ หน้า ๑๖๘ - ๑๘๒
———. *Phrabat*
ดำรงราชานุภาพ กรมพระ
อธิบายเรื่องพระบาท
ประชุมพระนิพนธ์เบ็ดเตล็ด พศ ๒๕๐๔ หน้า ๖๓ - ๗๖

———. *Phračedi sam ǫng*
ดำรงราชนุภาพ กรมพระ
วินิฉัยเรื่องพระเจดีย์สามองค์ in
ประชุมพระนิพนธ์เบ็ดเตล็ด พศ ๒๕๐๔ หน้า ๒๗ - ๓๖

———. *Prapheni prakat*
ดำรงราชนุภาพ กรมพระ
ประเพณีประกาศพระราชกฤษฎีกาแต่โบราณ in
ประชุมพระนิพนธ์เบ็ดเตล็ด พศ ๒๕๐๔ หน้า ๑๓๑ - ๑๓๖

———. *Phraprawat Somdet Phra Naresuon Maharat*
ดำรงราชานุภาพ
พระประวัติสมเด็จพระนเรศวรมหาราช พศ ๒๕๐๓

———. *Prawat athibǫdi song Wat Mahathat*
ดำรงราชนุภาพ กรมพระ
ประวัติอธิบดีสงค์วัดมหาธาตุ พศ ๒๔๘๖

———. *Ratchakan thi sǫng*
ดำรงราชนุภาพ กรมพระ
พระราชพงศาวดารกรุงรัตนโกสินทร์รัชกาลที่ ๒
พศ ๒๕๐๔

———. *Rüa rop Thai*
ดำรงราชนุภาพ กรมพระ
ตำนานเรือรบไทย พศ ๒๔๗๔

———. *Rüang thong Thai*
ดำรงราชนุภาพ กรมพระ
อธิบายเรื่องธงไทยการปกครองประเทศไทย
แต่โบราณและอักขรานุกรมศิลปากร พศ ๒๕๐๓

———. *Song phra ǫng*
ดำรงราชนุภาพ กรมพระ
เรื่องเมืองไทยมีพระเจ้าแผ่นดิน ๒ พระองค์ in
นิทานโบราณคดี พศ ๒๕๐๓ หน้า ๔๘๒ - ๕๑๒

———. *Tamnan kan thi Thai rien phasa angkrit*
ดำรงราชนุภาพ กรมพระ
ตำนานการที่ไทยเรียนภาษาอังกฤษ in
ประชุมพระนิพนธ์เบ็ดเตล็ด พศ ๒๕๐๔ หน้า ๑๐๓–๑๑๖

———. *Tamnan ken thahan*
ดำรงราชนุภาพ กรมพระ
ตำนานการเกณฑ์ทหารไทย
ประชุมพงศาวดาร ๒๓ หน้า ๑ - ๕๔

———. *Tamnan kotmai mŭang Thai*
ดำรงราชนุภาพ กรมพระ
ตำนานกฎหมายเมืองไทยและประมวลคำอธิบาย
ทางนิติศาสตร์ พศ ๒๕๐๓

———. *Tamnan loek bọnbie*
ดำรงราชนุภาพ กรมพระ
เรื่องตำนานการเลิกบ่อนเบี้ยแลเลิกหวย
ประชุมพงศาวดาร ๑๗

———. *Tamnan phasi akọn*
ดำรงราชนุภาพ กรมพระ
ตำนานภาษีอากรบางยาง in
ลัทธิธรรมเนียมตางๆ ภาคที่ ๑๖ พศ ๒๔๗๐

———. *Tamnan wang kau*
ดำรงราชนุภาพ กรมพระ
เรื่องตำนานวังเก่า ประชุมพงศาวดาร ๒๖

———. *Tamnan wang na*
ดำรงราชนุภาพ กรมพระ
ตำนานวังนา ประชุมพงศาวดาร ๑๓

———. *Thai rop Phama*
ดำรงราชนุภาพ กรมพระ
พงศาวดารเรื่องไทยรบพม่า
ประชุมพงศาวดาร ๖ (สองเล่ม)

———. *Wadui yot čau*

ดำรงราชนุภาพ กรมพระ

อธิบายว่าด้วยยศเจ้า in

ประชุมพระนิพนธ์เบ็ดเตล็ด พศ ๒๕๐๔ หน้า ๗๗ - ๑๐๒

———. *Winichai phrayot*

ดำรงราชนุภาพ กรมพระ

วินิฉัยพระยศเจ้านายที่เรียกว่ากรมสมเด็จหรือสมเด็จกรม in

ประชุมพระนิพนธ์เบ็ดเตล็ด พศ ๒๕๐๔ หน้า ๑ - ๒๖

———, Ratchasena. *Thetsaphiban*

ดำรงราชนุภาพ กรมพระ และ ราชเสนา พระยา

เทศาภิบาล พศ ๒๕๐๓

Dhani Nivat. *Phraphutha Yǫt Fa songfūnfu wathanathamm*

พิทยลาภพฤฒิยากร พระวรวงศ์เธอกรมหมื่น

พระบาทสมเด็จพระพุทธยอดฟ้าจุฬาโลกทรงฟื้นฟูวัฒนธรรม

พศ ๒๕๐๐

Ïeyaming-Phitsanakha. *Phra Čau Taksin Maharat*

เอี๊ยะมิ้ง และ พิศนาคะ

สมเด็จพระเจ้าตากสินมหาราช พศ ๒๔๙๙

Khamhaikan chau angwa

คำให้การชาวอังวะ

ประชุมพงศาวดาร ๑๔ หน้า ๑ - ๒๔

Khamhaikan Mahakho

คำให้การมหาโคมหากฤชเรื่องเมืองพะม่า

ประชุมพงศาวดาร ๑๔ หน้า ๒๕ - ๓๙

Khamhaikan Mūang Atapū

คำให้การเมืองอัตปือ

ประชุมพงศาวดาร ๗๐ หน้า ๒๒๐ - ๒๒๘

Khathathǫnthǫranin. *Phongsawadan Phratabǫng*

คทาธรธรณินทร เจ้าพระยา

พงศาวดารเมืองพระตะบอง

ประชุมพงศาวดาร ๑๖

Khun Khlon Khamhaikan

คำให้การขุนโขลนเรื่องพระพุทธบาท

ประชุมพงศาวดาร ๗ หน้า ๔๙ - ๖๓

Kosapan pai Farangset

โกษาปาน ไป ฝรั่งเศส

ประชุม พงศาวดาร ภาค ๕๗ ถึง ๖๐

Laksana kan phraratcha phithi sokan nai ratchtakan thi nüng

ลักษณะการพระราชพิธีโสกันต์ในรัชกาลที่ ๑ in

ลัทธิธรรมเนียมตางๆ พศ ๒๕๐๔ หน้า

๕๘๕ - ๖๕๒

Lingat. *Kham nam*

แลงกาตร

(คำนำของผู้จัดพิมพ์) ประมวลกฎหมาย

รัชกาลที่ ๑ ฆ - ญ

Mahāamatayathibǫdi. *Phongsawadan Chiengmai*

มหาอำมาตยาธิบดี พระยา

พงศาวดารเมืองนครเชียงใหม่เมืองนคร

ลำปางเมืองนครลำพูนไชย

ประชุมพงศาวดาร ๓ หนา ๗๔ - ๑๑๒

Mahanuphap. *Nirat pai müang Čin*

มหานุภาพ พระยา

นิราศไปเมืองจีนปีฉลู ๒๓๒๔ พศ ๒๕๐๓

Mahasurasinghanat. *Nirat Nakhọn Si Thammarat*

มหาสุรสิงหนาท กรมพระราชวังบวร
นิราศเสด็จไปปราบพม่าเมืองนครศรีธรรมราช
เมื่อปีมะเมีย พศ ๒๓๒๙
นิราศพระราชนิพนธ์กรมพระราชวังบวร
มหาสุรสิงหนาท พศ ๒๔๖๙ หน้า ๑ - ๑๗

———. *Nirat ti Phama*

มหาสุรสิงหนาท กรมพระราชวังบวร
เพลงยาวนิราศเสด็จไปตีเมืองพม่าเมื่อ พศ ๒๓๓๖
นิราศพระราชนิพนธ์กรมพระราชวังบวรมหาสุรสิงหนาท
พศ ๒๔๖๙ หน้า ๑๘ - ๓๐

———. *Phrabọwọnratcha prawat lae bọwọn ratcha niphon*

มหาสุรสิงหนาท กรมพระราชวังบวร
พระบวรราชประวัติแลพระบวรราชนิพนธ์ พศ ๒๔๘๑

Narinthewi. *Khuam songčam*

นรินเทวี กรมหลวง
จดหมายเหตุความทรงจำ พศ ๒๕๐๑

Nitisatphaisan. *Prawatsat kotmai Thai*

นิติศาสตร์ไพศาลย์ พระยา
ประวัติศาสตร์กฎหมายไทย พศ ๒๕๐๐

Pathom wong

เรื่องปฐมวงษ์พระราชนิพนธ์รัชกาลที่ ๔
ประชุมพงศาวดาร ๘ หน้า๘๖ - ๑๐๘

Phadung Khwaen Pračan. *Latthithammaniem ratsadọn phak Isan*

ผดุง แคว้น ประจันต์ หลวง
ลัทธิธรรมเนียมราษฎรภาคอีสาน in
ลัทธิธรรมเนียมตางๆ พศ ๒๕๐๔ หน้า ๕ - ๖๔

Phichai songkhram Thai

พิไชยสงครามไทยลอกมาจาก
ฉบับของหลวงเสนา

Phitsanakha. *Prawatsat kasat Thai*

พิศนาคะ

ประวัติศาสตร์กษัตริย์ไทย ๙ รัชกาล พศ ๒๕๐๐

Phongsawadan Kelantan

พงศาวดารกลันตัน

ประชุมพงศาวดาร ๒ หน้า ๑๑๗ - ๑๓๓

Phongsawadan Khamen

พงศาวดารเขมร

ประชุมพงศาวดาร ๑ หน้า ๑๖๕ - ๒๖๘

Phongsawadan Khamen yang yọ

พงศาวดารเขมรอย่างย่อ

ประชุมพงศาวดาร๗๑ หน้า ๙๕ - ๑๐๓

Phongsawadan Lan Chang

พงศาวดารเมืองล้านช้าง

ประชุมพงศาวดาร ๑ หน้า ๓๘๗ - ๔๓๒

Phongsawadan Luong Phra Bang

พงศาวดารเมืองหลวงพระบาง

ประชุมพงศาวดาร ๕ หน้า ๒๓๒ - ๒๗๘

Phongsawadan Mọn Phama

พงศาวดารมอญพม่า

ประชุมพงศาวดาร ๑ หน้า ๒๖๙ - ๓๘๖

Phongsawadan Phanom

พงศาวดารเมืองนครพนมสันเขป

ประชุมพงศาวดาร ๗๐ หน้า ๒๓๗ - ๒๔๖

Phongsawadan Phathalung

พงศาวดารเมืองพัทลุง

ประชุมพงศาวดาร ๕๓ หน้า ๑๒๘ - ๑๓๔

Phongsawadan Phraratchachatlekha

พระราชพงศาวดารฉบับพระราชหัตเลขา

เล่ม ๒ ตอน ๒ พศ ๒๔๙๕

Phongsawadan Saiburi

พงศาวดารเมืองไทรบุรี

ประชุมพงศาวดาร ๒ หน้า ๖๙ - ๑๐๐

Phongsawadan Thalang

พงศาวดาร เมืองถลาง

ประชุมพงศาวดาร ๒ หน้า ๕๖ - ๖๙

Phongsawadan Trangkanu

พงศวดารเมืองตรังกานู

ประชุมพงศาวดาร ๒ หน้า ๑๐๐ - ๑๑๗

Phongsawadan Yuon

พงศาวดารญวน

ประชุมพงศาวดาร ๒๘ หน้า ๑ - ๑๘

Phothiprasat. *Sathapatayakamm*

โพธิประสาท นารถ

สถาปตยกรรมในประเทศไทย พศ ๒๔๘๗

Phra nam phra orothida

พระนามพระโอรศธิดาในกรมพระราชวังบวร

มหาสุรสิงหนาทรัชกาลที่ ๑

ประชุมพงศาวดาร ๑๓ หน้า ๑๕๔ - ๑๙๗

Phraratchanukit

เรื่องพระราชนุกิจ พศ ๒๔๘๙

Phraratcha Phongsawadan Krung Thonburi

พระราชพงศาวดารกรุงธนบุรีแผ่นดินสมเด็จ

พระบรมราชาที่ ๔ (พระเจาตากสิน) รศ ๑๓๑

P.P. See *Phongsawadan Phraratchahatlekha.*

P.P.R.I. See Thiphakarawong, *Phraratcha Phongsawadan Rama I*

Prachakitčakoračak. *Phongsawadan Yonok*

ประชากิจกรจักร พระยา

หนังสือพงศาวดารโยนก พศ ๒๕๐๔

Prachum čarük Wat Phrachetuphon

ประชุมจารึกวัดพระเชตุพน เล่ม ๑ พศ ๒๔๗๒

Pramuon kotmai ratchakan thi nüng

ประมวลกฎหมายรัชกาลที่ ๑ จศ ๑๑๖๖

ตามฉบับหลวงตราสามดวง เล่ม ๑,๒,๓

Prawat sankhep phra čau Nakhon Si Thammarat

พระประวัติสันเขปพระเจ้านครศรีธรรมราช

ประชุมพงศาวดาร ๗๓ หน้า ๖๔ - ๑๐๔

Prawat wannakhadi Thai

เปลื้อง ณ นคร

ประวัติวรรณคดีไทย พศ ๒๕๐๓

Premčit. *Songkhram Thai Khamen*

เปรมจิตต์ สิริ

สงครามระหว่างไทยกับเขมรและปราสาทเขา

พระวิหารของไทย พศ ๒๕๐๓

Rama I. *Nirat . . . Tha Din Daeng*

พระราชนิพนธ์รัชกาลที่ ๑

กลอนเพลงยาวนิราศเรื่องรบพม่าที่ท่าดินแดง

พศ ๒๔๖๔

Ratchasakunwong

ราชสกูลวงศ์

พระนามเจ้าฟ้าและพระองค์เจ้าในกรุงรตนโกสินทร

พศ ๒๔๖๙

Rithirongrǫnachet. *Phongsawadan Mŭang Lai*

ฤทธิรงค์รณเฉท พระยา

พงศาวดารเมืองไล

ประชุมพงศาวดาร ๙ หน้า ๒๙ - ๗๗

Rithirǫngrǫnachet. *Phongsawadan Mŭang Thaeng*

ฤทธิรงค์รณเฉท พระยา

พงสาวดารเมืองแถง

ประชุมพงศาวดาร ๙

Rŭang kio kap krung kau

เรื่องเกี่ยวกับกรุงเก่า

ประชุมพงศาวดาร ๖๙

Senabǫdi mahatthai

เสนาบดีมหาดไทยนครบาล พศ ๒๔๗๗

Si Wǫrawat. *Phongsawadan Phathalung*

ศรีวรวัตร หลวง

พงศาวดารเมืองพัทลุงตั้งแต่สมัยดึกดำบรรพ์ถึง

สมัยปัจจุบัน

ประชุมพงศาวดาร ๑๕ หน้า ๑ - ๘๑

Sommot Amǫraphan. *Chaloem phrayot čau nai*

สมมตอมรพันธุ พระเจ้าบรมวงศ์เธอกรมพระ

เรื่องเฉลิมพระยศเจ้านาย พศ ๒๔๗๒

———. *Song tang phra bǫrǫmawongsanuwong*

สมมตอมรพนธุ์ พระเจ้าบรมวงศ์เธอกรมพระ

เรื่องทรงตั้งพระบรมวงศานุวงศ์กรุงรัตนโกสินทร

พศ ๒๔๖๘

———. *Tang čau phraya*

สมมตอมรพันธุ์ พระเจ้าบรมวงศ์เธอกรมพระ

เรื่องตั้งเจ้าพระยาในกรุงรัตนโกสินทร พศ ๒๔๖๑

Somphot phra nakhon khrop roi pi

สมโภชพระนครครบร้อยปี พศ ๒๕๐๓

Sonakun. *Prawatsat Thai samai krung ratanakosin yuk raek*

โสณกุล หม่อมเจ้าหญิง

ประวัติศาสตร์ไทยสมัยกรุงรัตนโกสินทร์ยุคแรก

พศ ๒๕๐๑

Sunthon Phithak. *Phlengyau rop phama thi Chiengmai*

พิทักษ สุนทร พยา

เพลงยาวเรื่องกรมพระราชวังบวรมหาสุรสิงหนาท

รบพม่าที่เมืองเชียงใหม่

Suriyaphong. *Phongsawadan Nan*

สุริยพงษผริตเดช พระเจา

เรื่องราชวงษปกรณ์พงศาวดารเมืองนาน

ประชุมพงศาวดาร ๑๐

Tamnan phra kot

ตำนานพระโกษฐ

ประชุมพงศาวดาร ๘ หน้า ๑๐๙ - ๑๒๐

Tamra krabuon sadet

ตำรากระบวนเสด็จและกระบวนแห่แต่โบราณ in

ลัทธิธรรมเนียมตางๆ พศ ๒๕๐๔ หน้า ๔๔๙ - ๕๔๘

Tang čau phraya Nakhon Si Thammarat

เรื่องตั้งเจ้าพระยานครศรีธรรมราช

ประชุมพงศาวดาร ๒ หน้า ๒ - ๕๖

Thiphakarawong. *Phraratcha Phongsawadan Rama I*

ทิพากรวงศ์ เจ้าพระยา

พระราชพงศาวดารรัชกาลที่ ๑ พศ ๒๕๐๓

Thut farang samai ratanakosin

เรื่องทูตฝรั่งสมัยรัตนโกสินทร

ประชุมพงศาวดาร ๖๒

Wanarat. *Thetsana*

วันรัต สมเด็จพระ

เทศนาบวรราชประวัติ

ประชุมพงศาวดาร ๑๓ หน้า ๑๒๘ - ๑๕๓

Wichienkhiri. *Phongsawadan Patani*

วิเชียนคิรี พระยา

พงศาวดารเมืองปัตตานี

ประชุมพงศาวดาร ๒ หน้า ๑ - ๒๙

———. *Phongsawadan Songkhla I*

วิเชียนคิรี พระยา

พงศาวดารเมืองสงขลา

ประชุมพงศาวดาร ๓ หน้า ๑๐ - ๗๓

———, *Phongsawadan Songkhla II*

วิเชียนคิรี เจ้าพระยา

พงศาวดารเมืองสงขลา

ประชุมพงศาวดาร ๕๓ หน้า ๑ - ๑๐๑

II. *Lao source*

Phongsawadan Lao

ພງສາວະດານລາວ

ກະຊວງສຶກສາທິການ

Vientiane 1957

III. *Literature in Western languages.*

Aymonier, E. *Le Cambodge*, vol. 3 (Paris, 1904).

Bowring, J. *The Kingdom and the People of Siam*, 2 vols. (London, 1857).

Buribhand, B. Luang, *The Buddha's Footprint* (Bangkok, 1955).

Cadière, L. "Documents Relatifs à l'Époque de Gia-Long," *Bulletin de l'École Française d'Extrême-Orient*, vol. 12, no. 7 (1412), pp. 1–82.

Chakrabongse, Prince Chula. *Lords of Life, The paternal monarchy of Bangkok, 1782–1932* (London, 1960).

Chumsai, M. *History of Laos*, typescript (Bangkok, 1960).

Coedès, G. *Les collections archéologiques du Musée National de Bangkok*, Ars Asiatica, no. 12 (Paris and Brussels, 1928).

———. *Les peuples de la péninsule indochinoise, histoire, Civilisations*, (Paris, 1962).

———. *The Vajirañāṇa National Library* (Bangkok, 1924).

Dhani Nivat, Prince. "The Inscriptions of Vat Jetubhon," *Journal of the Siam Society*, vol. 25, no. 2 (1933), pp. 143–170.

———. "The Old Siamese Conception of the Monarchy," *Journal of the Siam Society*, vol. 36, no. 2 (1947), pp. 91–106.

———. "The Ramakien: A Siamese Version of the Story of Rama," *Journal of the Burma Research Society* (Commemoration Number), vol. 1 (1960), pp. 33–45.

———. "The Reconstruction of Rama I of the Chakry Dynasty," *Journal of the Siam Society*, vol. 43, no. 1 (1955), pp. 21–47.

———. *The Royal Palaces* (Bangkok, 1963).

Döhring, K. *Buddhistische Tempelanlagen in Siam*, 3 vols. (Berlin, 1920).

Fairbank, J. K. and Teng, S. T. "On the Ch'ing Tributary System," *Harvard Journal of Asiatic Studies*, vol. 6 (1941), pp. 135–246.

Gosselin, Ch. *L'Empire d'Annam* (Paris, 1904).

Graham, W. A. *Kelantan* (Glasgow, 1908).

Hall, D. G. E. *A History of South-East Asia* (London, 1955).

Harrison, B. *South-East Asia, A Short History* (London, 1955).

Harvey, G. E. *History of Burma, From the Earliest Times to 10th. March 1824* (London, 1925).

Hutchinson, E. W. "A French Garrison at Bangkok, 1687–1688," *Journal of the Siam Society*, vol. 31, no. 2 (1939), pp. 119–135.

———. "Four French State Manuscripts," *Journal of the Siam Society*, vol. 27, no. 2 (1935), pp. 183–244.

Launay, A. *Histoire Ancienne et Moderne de l'Annam* (Paris, 1884).

———. *Histoire de la Mission de Siam, 1662–1811*, 2 vols. (Paris, 1920).

———. *Siam et les Missionaires Français* (Tours, 1896).

Le Boulanger, P. *Histoire du Laos Français* (Paris, 1931).

Leclère, A. *Histoire du Cambodge depuis le 1er siècle de notre ère* (Paris, 1915).

Lê Thánh Khôi. *Le Viet-Nam, Histoire et Civilisation* (Paris, 1955).

Lingat, R. "Evolution of the Conception of Law in Burma and Siam," *Journal of the Siam Society*, vol. 38, no. 1 (1950), pp. 9–31.

———. "Le Culte du Bouddha d'Émeraude," *Journal of the Siam Society*, vol. 27, no. 1 (1934), pp. 9–38.

Lingat, R. "Note sur la Révision des Lois Siamoises en 1805," *Journal of the Siam Society*, vol. 23, no. 1 (1929), pp. 19–27.

McNair, J. F. A. *Perak and the Malays* (London, 1878).

Maha Sila Viravong. *History of Laos*, mimeographed (New York, 1958; reprinted 1964).

Masao, T. "Researches into Indigenous Law of Siam as a Study of Comparative Jurisprudence," *Journal of the Siam Society*, vol. 2, no. 1 (1905), pp. 14–18.

Masson, A. *Histoire de l'Indochine* (Paris, 1950).

Maybon, Ch. B. *Histoire Moderne du Pays d'Annam* (Paris, 1920).

Mills, L. A. "British Malaya," *Journal of the Malayan Branch of the Royal Asiatic Society*, vol. 3, no. 2 (1925), pp. 1–340.

Moura, Jacinto José do Nascimento. "Relaçoes dos Portugueses com o Sião," *Boletim das Agencia Geral das Colonias*, vol. 3, no. 68 (1931), pp. 35–55; vol. 7, no. 69 (1931), pp. 52–57.

Notton, C. (trans.). *The Chronicle of the Emerald Buddha* (Bangkok, 1933, 2nd ed.).

Phayre, A. *History of Burma* (London, 1883).

Phraison Salarak, Luong. "Intercourse between Burma and Siam, as Recorded in Hmannan Yazawindawgyi," *Journal of the Siam Society*, vol. 13, no. 1 (1919), pp. 1–65.

Quaritch-Wales, H. G. *Ancient Siamese Government and Administration* (London, 1934).

———. *Ancient South-East Asian Warfare* (London, 1952).

———. *Siamese State Ceremonies* (London, 1931).

Rentse, A. "History of Kelantan I," *Journal of the Malayan Branch of the Royal Asiatic Society*, vol. 12 (1934), pp. 44–62.

Robert-Martignan, L. *La Monarchie Absolue Siamoise de 1350 à 1926* (Cannes, 1939).

Sangermano, Father. *A Description of the Burmese Empire* (Rome, 1883).

Shideler, J. "Mapping Thailand," *Bangkok World*, July 22, 1962, pp. 2–4.

Skinner, W. S. *Chinese Society in Thailand* (Ithaca and New York, 1957).

Smith, M., *A Physician at the Court of Siam*, London, 1946.

Sternstein, L. "An Historical Atlas of Thailand," *Journal of the Siam Society*, vol. 52, no. 1 (1964), pp. 7–20.

Swettenham, T. F. *British Malaya* (London, 1920).

Symes, M. *An Account of an Embassy to the Kingdom of Ava . . . in the year 1795*, 3 vols. (London, 1800, 2nd ed.).

Taboulet, G. *La Geste Française en Indochine* (Paris, 1955, tome premier).

Tarling, N. "British Policy in the Malay Peninsula and Archipelago, 1824–1871," *Journal of the Malayan Branch of the Royal Asiatic Society*, vol. 30 (1957), 3, pp. 1–228.

Vella, W. F. *Siam under Rama III, 1824–1851* (Locust Valley, New York, 1957).

———. "The Impact of the West on the Government of Thailand," *University of California Publications in Political Science*, vol. 4, no. 3 (1955), pp. 317–410.

Wenk, K. *Die Verfassungen Thailands* (Frankfurt-am-Main, 1964).

———. "Prăchum Phongsāwadān, Ein Beitrag zur Bibliographie der thailändischen historischen Quellen," *Oriens Extremus*, vol. 9, no. 2 (1962), pp. 232–257.

Winstedt, R. O. "A History of Malaya," *Journal of the Malayan Branch of the Royal Asiatic Society*, vol. 13, no. 1 (1935), pp. 1–270.

Winstedt-Wilkinson. "A History of Perak," *Journal of the Malayan Branch of the Royal Asiatic Society*, vol. 12, no. 1 (1934), pp. 1–180.

Wood, W. A. R. *A History of Siam* (Bangkok, 1933, rev. ed.).

Wyatt, J. N. "Siam and Laos, 1767–1824," *Journal Southeast Asian History*, vol. 4, no. 2 (1963), pp. 19–47.

INDEX